TALKING TEACHING
with the
DYNAMIC DEPUTIES

TALKING
TEACHING
with the
DYNAMIC
DEPUTIES

★ inspiring CPD for every teacher ★

RUSSELL PEARSON · STEVEN EASTES

CORWIN

A SAGE company
2455 Teller Road
Thousand Oaks, California 91320
(0800)233-9936
www.corwin.com

SAGE Publications Ltd
1 Oliver's Yard
55 City Road
London EC1Y 1SP

SAGE Publications India Pvt Ltd
B 1/I 1 Mohan Cooperative Industrial /
Mathura Road
New Delhi 110 044

SAGE Publications Asia-Pacific Pte Ltd
3 Church Street
#10-04 Samsung Hub
Singapore 049483

Editor: Amy Thornton
Senior project editor: Chris Marke
Cover design: Wendy Scott
Typeset by: C&M Digitals (P) Ltd, Chennai, India
Printed in the UK

Library of Congress Control Number: 2021947640

British Library Cataloguing in Publication Data

A catalogue record for this book is available
from the British Library.

ISBN 978-1-5297-7721-5
ISBN 978-1-5297-7720-8 (pbk)

At SAGE we take sustainability seriously. Most of our products are printed in the UK using responsibly sourced
papers and boards. When we print overseas we ensure sustainable papers are used as measured by the PREPS
grading system. We undertake an annual audit to monitor our sustainability.

CONTENTS

ABOUT THE AUTHORS

Russell and Steve (the *Dynamic Deputies*) are Primary Deputy Headteachers who worked together between 2012 and 2015. During this time, they would often have rich conversations about all things teaching and leadership. Despite Russell's relocation to Devon in 2015, these discussions continued in the form of their podcast *Don't Shoot the Deputies* (now called *The Dynamic Deputies Podcast*), an idea that occurred to Steve in the summer of 2018.

Russell is particularly interested in curriculum design, mathematics and the wellbeing of the school community. After studying for an English Literature degree at Roehampton University, he completed a PGCE at Canterbury Christchurch, where he specialised in History. Russell has since worked in four primary schools. He has been a Maths Lead (and SLE), an Assessment Coordinator, an Assistant Head, and is now enjoying life as a Deputy Headteacher. He lives with his wife and two daughters in South Devon, sandwiched between Dartmoor and the coast.

Steve is passionate about the effective training and coaching of staff, and how leaders can best equip their colleagues to deliver an inspiring education. Initially studying criminal law, Steve's work took him to Melbourne, Australia. After five and a half years as a solicitor, he was drawn to a career in education, inspired by his mum (a Teaching Assistant for many years). Steve also completed a PGCE at Canterbury Christchurch, before working for many years at a school in Kent, working his way up from NQT to Deputy Headteacher. Before becoming a Deputy Head, Steve was an ICT Coordinator, a Key Stage Leader and also did a brief stint as an Assistant Head alongside Russell. He lives in Canterbury with his partner and their three children.

INTRODUCTION

Hello and welcome to *Talking Teaching with the Dynamic Deputies*, a book written by two Deputy Heads living on opposite sides of the country. Let us give you some background about how this venture came about.

We used to really enjoy working together, particularly around the time that we had both taken on new leadership roles in the same school. There was a powerful camaraderie generated by each of us facing the same challenges that new leaders inevitably encounter. During our weekly leadership time, we'd talk through our issues, we'd collaborate, we'd strategise and we'd problem-solve together. We learnt about how to manage our colleagues' varying needs, how to provide feedback and how to put school priorities into action. In hindsight, we're certain that we made plenty of mistakes during this time, but we also think we did some pretty good stuff, too. Our Headteacher felt that we made an effective partnership and affectionately nicknamed us the 'Dynamic Duo'. This is where the 'Dynamic Deputies' name came from a few years later.

Russell's relocation to Devon in 2015 was rather disruptive to our dynamic partnership. Nevertheless, life went on and we each stepped into more senior roles. It was difficult for both of us not to have that close friend to talk to about work, but we continued to send the odd text and words of encouragement to one another.

Then, in the summer of 2018, a little text exchange occurred. Something along the lines of:

Steve: Russell. I've had an idea.
Russell: Uh-oh.
Steve: Why don't we start up a podcast? And a Facebook group for teachers? And a Twitter page? That way we can keep talking about work stuff.
Russell: Sounds fun. Let's do it.

In all honesty, neither of us really understood what a podcast was at that time, nor had we ever listened to one. We knew the basic idea: you chatted about something, you recorded it, you posted it online and then you hoped people would listen. What did we have to lose?

Fast-forward a few years and here we are. We have recorded dozens of episodes and have spoken to a diverse range of educators from all over the country. We have always followed our guts with the podcast, choosing to speak to people who we are drawn to because of their expertise and the quality of their character. It has been the most phenomenal example of self-generated CPD, and we are in no doubt that we are the teachers and leaders we are today because of it. It is the gift that keeps on giving.

In late 2020, we talked about the idea of writing a book. We thought about how great it would be to be able to capture some of the learning we'd experienced so that we could share this wealth of knowledge with other educators, whatever their level of experience. We were therefore delighted when the opportunity arose not long after this conversation.

Talking Teaching with the Dynamic Deputies: Inspiring CPD for Every Teacher is based on ten themes that are pertinent for everyone working in education. The inspiration for each chapter is an interview we recorded for the podcast. In each chapter, the relevant guests will introduce themselves to you in their own words before we then summarise some of the key points of learning from the interview using some of our favourite quotations from the episode. We will then go on to reflect further on the theme at hand, with each of us offering our own reflections and linking this to our personal experiences in school. Finally, the chapter will close with some reflective points that you may wish to think about on a personal level or that you may like to use within a CPD session at your school.

The aim of this book is to leave you feeling uplifted and inspired. We have so much to learn from other teachers and leaders in this profession. This book is a celebration of just some of the incredible wisdom and expertise that is out there. We want to say a huge thank you to all the guests who agreed to be featured in this book – you are all incredible.

CHAPTER 1

EVERYDAY HEROES

LINKED PODCAST EPISODE:
*Jaz Ampaw-Farr – Everyday
Heroes*

GUEST:
Jaz Ampaw-Farr

IN THIS CHAPTER WE EXPLORE:

- the difference teachers make to young people;
- the value of relationships in schools;
- the power of high expectations.

ABOUT ME: JAZ AMPAW-FARR

Statistically speaking, someone with a story of poverty, foster care and life on the streets doesn't find themselves going on to do their dream job as a teacher. They don't tend to have a career as an international keynote speaker, or necessarily have their own loving family that they're actually happy to be 'locked down' with. But I did, and that's all because of everyday heroes, just like you. Five teachers in particular met me where I was and gave me what we all need more than anything else: an authentic and consistent human connection.

As a teacher, I was passionate about reading, writing and spelling, so I set up my own consultancy business. After the birth of my first child, I went on to advise governments, leaders and teachers around the world. By the time my second child came along, I'd been invited by the DfE to work alongside Sir Jim Rose (the Oprah of phonics). I continued to speak, train and advise on literacy, but when my third child arrived, I decided to sit down for a bit. I started contributing to *TES* and other educational periodicals and co-authored a series of three research papers, too.

Along the way, I've been a TV presenter, a stand-up comedian and a motivational keynote speaker. I also wrote a book, *Because of You, This is Me*. The pandemic saw me pivot and focus on delivering digital keynotes on human-first leadership, resilience, bias, wellbeing and communication to a mixture of educational and corporate organisations.

This incredible journey would not have been possible without the difference that teachers made in my life. Dealing with imposter syndrome and self-doubt has been a mammoth effort, and I've had to continually embed the ambitious resilience I talk to others about on a daily basis. My ultimate goal is to amplify the voices of the most important people on the planet – educators.

JAZ AMPAW-FARR: THE INTERVIEW

Welcome to Jaz Ampaw-Farr, one of the most incredible human beings we've ever met. A witty, compassionate and forward-looking change-maker, Jaz specialises in reminding any teacher who will listen that they make an extraordinary difference each and every day.

We interviewed Jaz in May 2020, right in the midst of the first national lockdown. We were looking to speak to someone who could lift our listeners' spirits during a terribly challenging time and Jaz didn't disappoint. She told us about her very difficult and distressing childhood, and about how her life could have panned out so differently from the way it has done. Yet somehow, five teachers in particular helped Jaz to recognise her true potential and gave her a glimpse into a happier future. These teachers provided Jaz with the guidance, support and high expectations she needed in order to strive for something bigger and better.

This chapter is about helping you to see something deeply and profoundly special about the work that you do. As Jaz says: 'you are an everyday hero'.

> *Schools have shown themselves for what they always were: so much more than academic institutions.*

There's no question: we're in the business of helping children to learn. It's essential that we do everything we can to help children to get good grades and to succeed academically. We know that a rich knowledge base and good qualifications can help to transform the life chances of the young people in our care (we'll explore this more later, in Chapter 8, Knowledge is Power). But whether we like it or not, we have a much greater influence on young people than that. In the podcast, Jaz had us think more deeply about the work that schools do. In the midst of a pandemic, we saw something quite profound about the role of our schools: we were truly the centre of our communities. We provided emotional support to parents, carers and their children, we delivered food parcels and exercise books, and we had truly unique insights into the lives our pupils were actually living. Jaz's point was that the pandemic simply shone a light on the fact that we were *always* much more than academic institutions. We've always done so much more than deliver great teaching.

What Jaz is talking about in this interview is the importance of having a human-first approach to the work that we do. She is calling on us to look at every parent, carer and child and see first that they are a person – a unique human being in need of our understanding, empathy and compassion. If indeed our influence is so much greater than the lessons that we teach, then what else is it that we can do to make such a difference to young people? Should we really be expected to have to do more than teach good lessons?

> *It's the glimmers of light, the smiles, it's the smallest acts of kindness. It's the true connection people make . . . it's the assuming the best rather than assuming the worst.*

We know very well what it is like to work as a teacher or leader in a busy school environment. We live much of our time 'up in our heads', processing our endless to-do lists and thinking about the next item we need to tick off. To a certain extent, we need to work like this, otherwise we might never keep on top of the workload. But in our haste to get 'the next thing' done, do we sometimes forget to be truly present for the colleagues and children we're sharing the building with? What might we be missing when we forget to live more mindfully at work?

For Jaz, her five everyday heroes didn't do anything overtly special. They were heroes because of the subtle things they did, that perhaps many of Jaz's other teachers didn't do. They took the time to notice her for the individual she was, and this wasn't an act that they would put on each day when they came to work. Quite simply: they genuinely cared about her, and from that place of caring came the compassionate behaviours that meant so much to the vulnerable young person that Jaz was at the time. Think back to your own schooling for one moment. Can you remember a particular teacher's smile or a moment when they showed you compassion? What did it feel like when they demonstrated that warmth and kindness? What did it do for your sense of emotional security or your desire to work hard for them? There is a magic that happens when we treat one another with a human-first approach. We see beyond each other's egos and behaviours, and straight to the true nature of the individual. In the natural smiles and words of kindness that Jaz's teachers showed her, they recognised something meaningful about who she was as an individual. And, most importantly, so did she.

Jaz's point about teachers assuming the best in pupils is extremely important, too. Have you ever felt unfairly judged or wrongly accused? As an adult, this is hard enough, but can you remember what it felt like as a child? Every one of us can think of a time when our character has been called into question – and, frankly, it's horrible. In the episode, Jaz called on us to assume the best of our pupils. This seems so simple that it is very easy to overlook the power of its implications. Thinking back again to your own teachers at school, did you sense which ones were all too ready to spot your every mistake? Some of you might recognise that you even ended up *enacting* their perception of you, almost as if you were fulfilling their vision of what kind of child you were. Yet, how different was it when a teacher saw you for who you truly were and worked hard to see the best in you? Did this affect how you reciprocated in terms of effort and respect? Sometimes what we all need is someone to see the potential in us – the potential that we might struggle to see without an everyday hero.

> Mrs Cook used to ask us: 'Who are you going to be when you grow up?'; not 'What are you going to do?' but 'Who are you going to be?'

In the podcast, Jaz talks about one teacher in particular, Mrs Cook, who decides to ask the children one day who they are going to be when they are older. Jaz panics, spouting out, 'I want to be just like you!' Mrs Cook doesn't let this compliment turn her all 'mushy', but responds by confidently affirming the idea that Jaz *will* be an educator one day and a great one at that. As Jaz recalled this event, she said: 'The way she looked at me made me feel like it was a done deal. It was like she tied this gold rope around my waist and hammered the other end into a stake 20 years into the future.' You see, children need their teachers to envisage a world in which they are a roaring success. Maybe some children need this more than others, but its power is phenomenal. Perhaps you've even experienced this feeling as an adult – a leader or colleague telling you what you are capable of or what you could go on to do one day in your career. We've both had people do that for us over the years, and there's no doubt that it truly expands your mental model of what you think you can achieve.

I'm talking about being professionally vulnerable and personally authentic. It is not what you get paid for and it's not in the teacher standards.

One of our favourite parts of the episode was when Jaz unpacked what some of these everyday heroes were like. She says: 'They weren't my kind of people . . . they were very straight, very kind of introverted, not very expressive . . . all the kind of aspects I wouldn't connect with. So it's not about personality.' You see, Jaz isn't calling for teachers to *act* like super heroes or to put on a persona that we *think* pupils will like. She's not asking you to befriend your students, pretend to understand the latest trend or to know everything about their home lives. She's asking us to be genuine and authentic in the work that we do. As we'll explore more in Chapter 3 on wellbeing, there is something incredibly infectious about being around people who are unashamedly 'themselves', and it seems to have us reconnect with our own true nature. Yet sometimes, as teachers, we can feel as if we need to put on a kind of front for our students. We're sorry to break it to you, but young people see straight through this. They know when we're 'faking it' or trying to be something we are not. So when we turn up for work, how about we just be ourselves and meet the students where they truly are? Jaz isn't asking for us to pour our hearts out to our students, but she is inviting us to let our natural humanity shine in our classrooms. Even if you have completely separate interests and a very different personality from your students, they will be drawn to your authenticity and this will make them feel more emotionally secure in your company.

It is the consistency, the authenticity and the embedded high expectations.

A lot is said in schools these days about ACEs (Adverse Childhood Experiences) and many people argue that it is essential that we have a basic understanding about the impact that ACEs can have on children in school. When we asked Jaz about her opinion on this, she said that our greatest offer to all pupils are ACE relationships:

- **A**uthenticity
- **C**onsistency
- (High) **E**xpectations embedded.

Jaz doesn't suggest that it is our role to unpick and analyse childhood trauma. As well as being authentically human, we need to be really consistent. As a child, Jaz benefited from being around adults who were reliable. Her everyday heroes didn't have rules and boundaries that shifted on a daily basis. Their warmth wasn't there one day and gone the next. She knew what to expect from them, and that made her feel secure. These everyday heroes also had extremely high expectations. There is a temptation, particularly when working with vulnerable pupils, to lower our expectations because we feel sympathy for them. Is this truly in our students' interests? As Jaz says about her everyday heroes: 'They didn't let me off.'

Instead, Jaz got this message from her teachers: 'I believe in you and there's nothing you can do to change that.' Jaz is making the point here that the everyday heroes in her life helped her to imagine a better version of herself by having full faith in her potential. They didn't have a 'bless her' approach. They told her – in fact, *insisted* – that she was going to be somebody. Is there a greater gift that we can offer a young person than this?

RUSSELL'S REFLECTION

Throughout my career, I've worked in schools with significant numbers of children who have experienced Adverse Childhood Experiences. Why have I continually chosen to work in such environments? I guess I am drawn to these children and their families because it gives me a deeper sense of fulfilment in the work that I do. I am obsessed with delivering a first-class education and creating the conditions that really enable pupils to improve their life chances. What gets me up each day is the prospect of helping young people to picture better and brighter futures than perhaps the existing ones they might imagine for themselves.

When I first started teaching, working in these kinds of schools weighed heavily on me emotionally. I have always found that children tend to feel safe to talk to me, to open up and share their worries. This is a huge privilege, of course, but I was never quite sure if I responded in a helpful way or not, and would often spend my evenings worrying about the children I was teaching. One thing I think I always did quite well was not to pass any judgement on the child, or their families, when I discovered some concerning information. Who was I to look down my nose at the lived experiences of young people or their parents? I think a lot of children who stay quiet about their experiences do so because of a fear that they will be judged.

In my first few years of teaching, I had children in my classes who:

- had parents who were alcoholics;
- disclosed stories of abuse to me;
- were living amidst domestic violence;
- had to tolerate constant arguing between separated parents;
- were living with adults suffering with mental health issues.

This has never really changed, either. I suspect many of you reading, just like me, sometimes feel quite overwhelmed by the scale of these issues and feel a bit helpless. But after talking to Jaz, and through my own personal growth, I've come to see that there is a much more hopeful picture for young people when we focus less on the trauma and more on creating the right conditions for them to thrive in school.

It's hard to remember how I responded to vulnerable students when I was 22 or 23, but I suspect I listened attentively, and perhaps even attempted to help them to understand how their experiences were affecting them now. I probably perceived these children as damaged and in need of fixing. Innocently, I may not have been helping my pupils by seeing them this way. I no longer see any young person as 'broken'.

Of course, our number one duty as educators is to safeguard our pupils. I hope it goes without saying that my first course of action would always be to follow my school's safeguarding procedures if a child disclosed a story of harm or abuse. But in terms of the ongoing pastoral work that I do with young people, I now tend to focus less on the past and more on the future. My focus is on pointing out the resilience and potential that I see in the young people I support in school. I can think of one incredible young person who I've worked with who has been through so much difficulty in their life. I've come to see that my best offer to them is to provide a stable, predictable structure at school where they can do well and thrive in their education. When we talk about their lived experiences, my tone is always as follows:

> We can't change the stuff you've gone through. It's horrible, and upsetting, and you didn't deserve any of it. But when we talk, I want to focus on what kind of human being you want to be. What do you want to achieve in your life? What can we do now to start you on a journey towards that place?

This is a shift from a focus on the past to one on the future. It's about helping young people to see that they do have some agency. Of course, any child who has experienced trauma has a right to feel let down, angry, anxious and so on. They also have a right to be protected from harm. But I've come to see that my best offer as an educator (who is not a counsellor) is to help them to focus on the things that are within their remit to influence. I don't want to fall into the trap of making excuses for students because I feel sorry for them. Just like Mrs Cook, I want to help them realise what they are capable of. I will never dismiss their lived experiences and I will, of course, make reasonable adjustments where needed. But it is my duty as an educator to help every child I serve to envisage their potential and give them the tools to achieve it.

Imagine being that child who has lived through some really tough stuff. Perhaps you were that child. And now imagine that the same child goes to school each day, only to find that every adult who speaks to them does so in such a way that empowers them to believe that their future success is absolutely possible. That's the kind of school I work in and the kind of place I will always want to be.

STEVE'S REFLECTION

This wonderful, uplifting and inspiring podcast was a reminder to me that teachers really can change lives. In fact, Jaz's story is testament to the fact that sometimes, in the most extreme cases, we may even *save* lives. Just take a moment to let that sink in: recognise that you *do* matter so much to the children you work with. Beyond the lesson plans, the endless data and the books we mark, we make incredible connections and find a 'way in' to build trusting relationships with the children in our schools. This human-first approach is the foundation of everything we do.

Before embarking on my teaching career, I worked as a family and criminal law solicitor in a rather deprived part of Kent. I worked with many so-called 'broken' families and extremely vulnerable children who were exposed to the horrors of this world on a daily basis. I vividly remember a day in court when my heart was breaking for a child I was working with. They turned to me and said that they would sing 'I'm Still Standing' by Elton John every night to remind them how strong they were – a resilient little person to say the least. Why am I telling you this? Because children and young adults *are* incredibly resilient, but they still need everyday heroes (just like you) to nurture them and to be that 'go-to' person they can share their life experiences with. It was a desire to support young people like this that drew me to want to be a teacher.

As a newly qualified teacher, I went into my first year hoping to be a friend for the children in my class. I hoped the children would like me and, as a result, perhaps they would behave for me. I soon realised that hope doesn't get you there on its own – you have to invest time in your relationships over a sustained period. I realised that for some children this could take a lot longer than I anticipated – perhaps the adults in their life weren't always easy to trust. Hearing Jaz talk about the teachers who were consistently reliable and who enabled her to see what she is capable of is inspirational — and something I would have loved to hear as a fresh face in the profession. Yes, you can be fun and enjoy the time with your class (that is a perk of the job), but being a strong role model with high expectations – no matter what circumstance the child finds themselves in – is so much more important. I can think of many children I have taught across the years who have frequently arrived at school late (for whatever reason), entering the building looking emotional and within minutes becoming disruptive. These children *need* you, and they need a relationship where they can feel comfortable and confident that you will listen to them, expect the best of them and be a safety blanket.

So how do we build these professional, trusting relationships with our pupils? First of all, let's recognise that it isn't just the most vulnerable children we are talking about. It is *every* child, of every presentation and from every walk of life who needs an everyday hero. In particular, I can think of the 'quiet types' in every class I've taught – you know, the 'silent majority' who can spend a day in your classroom without being noticed much at all? These children really need a relationship where their teachers know the little things about them – some of those small details about their lives that mean so much to them. When we make time to listen, it is from this place that connections can be made and from there we can go about raising expectations and building aspiration.

It is my experience that children will work harder for you if they have a bond with you. Not only will they be more likely to do well academically, but, most importantly, they will feel safer, happier and have more self-belief. So, take every opportunity you can to talk to the children you work with, be interested in their lives and build on it one step at a time. It could be as simple as remembering their favourite hobby, which perhaps you'll mention a few times a week. For example, I once had a very timid young boy in a Year 3 class. As I took those small steps to build a relationship with him, I found out that he loved judo, and he even went on to represent England. I fear that if I hadn't taken the time to talk to him (which never felt like hard work), then I could have gone a whole year without knowing about this huge part of his identity. It is also in simply noticing other little things that we truly connect with children. This might include praising them for the small accomplishments they achieve or in noticing that one piece of work where they had clearly tried that little bit harder.

What a privilege and an honour it is to be an everyday hero for young people. Whether we like it or not, the young people we serve need us for more than just the well-taught lessons. By slowly building trusting relationships, we provide a healthy model for their future relationships and, importantly, we empower them to achieve.

YOUR REFLECTION

Take some time to digest what you've read during this chapter. We have provided some question prompts that you may like to consider, depending on your current role or level of experience.

Support staff

- Are there any children you can think of who you haven't spoken to for a while? Perhaps you can think of a few quieter individuals who easily go unnoticed. How could you show them this week that you are interested in them and what they have to say?
- Are there any children who you've fallen into the habit of mainly noticing for negative reasons? This can easily happen to any of us, but may lead to a negative cycle forming. How could you shift this dynamic in the weeks ahead so that they know that you're looking for the positives?
- Think about the language you use with your less confident pupils. What sort of things might you say to your nervous pupils to raise their aspirations?

Trainee teachers

- During your placements, you'll realise that some children easily get the lion's share of your attention. How can you make sure that you get to know those quieter characters in the class as well?
- Examples of positive relationships while training are great to talk about in future interviews. Can you think of an example of where building trust with a vulnerable pupil helped you to teach them more effectively? If so, make a note of this and store it away for when the job-hunting begins.
- Take as many opportunities as you can to watch other teachers' interactions with their students. Which teachers seem to really connect with their pupils? What is it about the way they talk or listen to children that you can try to embed in your own practice?

Teachers

- Thinking about the pupils you currently teach, are there any young people you don't really know anything meaningful about? How about identifying one or two children right now who you are going to make that extra effort for in the weeks ahead?

- Remember when Jaz mentioned high expectations? Can you think of any vulnerable pupils who you make excuses for and inadvertently allow to underperform? What can you do in the weeks ahead to break this cycle? It might be that you need to look again at your expectations for behaviour or the standard of work you are accepting from them.
- Never underestimate the power of good relationships with parents/carers, as these people have a much bigger influence over your students' attitudes than you. Could you make the time for a positive phone call with the parent of a vulnerable pupil this week? Simple acts like this can help to improve parent attitudes towards school, which will only serve to benefit the young people we are supporting.

Senior leaders

- How visible have you been around the school lately? Making enough time for those little conversations with the children can be tough with all your other demands, but how does it shift your experience of school life? Remember that seeing and speaking to you will make many children feel hugely valued.
- Could you commit a regular time to getting out into classes and engaging more directly with the children? What might some of the benefits be of doing this consistently each week? Make sure you vary the classes you visit and make the effort to notice the little things that mean a lot to the children – e.g. their improved handwriting or a piece of work they are proud of.
- Are you playing a particularly pastoral role for any vulnerable children in school at the moment? If so, how can you frame your conversations with them to be about the bright future you envisage for them? What could the impact be if that young person hears one or two positive affirmations from you on a weekly basis? That could equate to almost one hundred encouraging interactions a year!

CHAPTER 2

COMMUNITY AND BELONGING

LINKED PODCAST EPISODE:
A Trip to Parklands, Leeds

GUEST:
Chris Dyson

IN THIS CHAPTER WE EXPLORE:

- what it means to belong to a school community;
- the impact of all staff and children feeling as if they truly belong;
- the importance of valuing the contribution all stakeholders make;
- how we might foster a sense of community within our classrooms.

ABOUT ME: CHRIS DYSON

It might surprise people to know that I didn't enter the world of teaching with a dream of changing lives. Growing up, I loved the outdoors and would spend endless hours outside with nothing but a tennis ball or a football. Teaching seemed like a good career option for me – I'd still be able to get outside a lot of the time and the holidays were great, too.

Since becoming a primary teacher, I've never looked back. I quickly realised that relationships were everything and, at one school, I ran an after-school club every day so that I could get to know my pupils better. In 2003, I was fortunate to be voted the *TES* Teacher of the Year – a huge privilege and an immensely proud moment for me. I absolutely loved being a teacher, and when the opportunities started arising to step into leadership, I wanted to remain in the classroom as much as possible.

After a brilliant experience as a Deputy Head, a headship came up at Parklands Primary School in Seacroft, one of the most deprived areas of the country. The local authority had described the school as 'requiring improvement' and results were heading south. People worried about me doing my first headship there, but what did I have to lose when it was failing anyway? I could bring my own ideas and vision, and, if it didn't work out, I could always go back to being a deputy. Thanks to my amazing mum, I'm a very caring person and I wanted to create a school culture built on love and respect. It took some time to change that culture at Parklands, but the same team that felt they were no good helped me to lead the school to a vote of 'outstanding' in 2017.

Growing up, we didn't have much, but I always say: what we lacked in money we made up for in love. As a headteacher, this is my same philosophy. When it comes to love, the kids at Parklands are some of the richest people in the world.

CHRIS DYSON: THE INTERVIEW

In March 2019, not long after beginning his first deputy headship, Russell was fortunate enough to visit Parklands Primary School in Leeds, alongside his Headteacher. The idea for the visit came from reading a blog on Twitter by @Southgloshead that depicted his own visit. He described a school that sounded truly magical and Russell was keen to see it for himself.

The Headteacher of Parklands Primary School is Chris Dyson, an inspirational leader who has taken the school on an incredible journey. It has gone from being a low-performing school to being one of the top-achieving primary schools in England. Chris nicknames his school 'The Fun Palace', and when you get there, you can see why. It is a school where joy is at the heart of everyday daily life. When you walk through the doors as a visitor, you're greeted with an enormous warm hug from Chris, while the sound of positive music blares out in the foyer outside his office. You immediately feel welcome and you instantly feel that you are part of the school community.

There are probably hundreds (if not thousands) of educators in schools who have been taught that you raise standards by 'being tough' and by not showing too much warmth. Chris's outlook flies in the face of this approach. He believes that you get the best out of children and staff when you are truly inclusive and when you treat people well. This means having a flexible approach for staff who are also parents, days in lieu for those who help with residentials and welcoming children who've been excluded from other settings. For Russell, seeing this philosophy in action was truly inspirational and gave him a better sense of what kind of school leader he might go on to be.

During a visit to Parklands, you actually spend very little time with Chris. After a brief chat with him, you are collected from his office by a couple of his pupils who proudly show you around their school and answer all your questions. You're given the space to meander, to ask difficult questions and to speak to any other staff or children you want to. Thankfully, over a cup of tea, Russell stole a few minutes to interview Chris about his school.

Nobody misses a Friday!

Every Friday at Parklands Primary, there are two assemblies: the 'calm' one in the morning and the 'noisy' one in the afternoon. Chris is rightly enormously proud of these assemblies and sees them as an essential ingredient in the school's success. During these assemblies, there are awards, singing, dancing and times-table competitions (among other activities). It is truly a sight to behold. During the interview, Russell asked Chris about the assemblies. Chris talked about the fact that no child ever wants to miss them and told the story of a girl who fractured her arm at playtime, but refused to go home because she didn't want to miss the afternoon assembly!

What is it about the assemblies at Parklands that means so much to the staff and children? Well, in our eyes it is the incredible sense of belonging that Chris has fostered. This is a time when the school comes together and unites to celebrate all that is good in that building. Many schools have a similar kind of assembly on a Friday, but the assemblies at Parklands are unparalleled for their positivity and feel-good energy. What is also so amazing to see is the sincere warmth and kindness the children show one another when awards are handed out. When a student's name is read out for an award, their peers are so incredibly proud of them that they end up being high-fived and hugged all the way to the front of the hall. It is like watching a celebrity navigating the red carpet and Chris calls it 'the walk of love'. The 'love' doesn't just come from the pupils' own classmates either; we're also talking about the children in other year groups, too – all desperate to congratulate their peers and show them some appreciation.

This begs the question: how do you go about getting your pupils to care so much for one another? It seems to us that like all other positive behaviours in schools, it's about constant modelling and having relentlessly high expectations. Chris and his team show the children what caring relationships look like at every opportunity. During a visit, you will see Chris's authentic and unwavering warmth towards his colleagues and children, whether that occurs through words of encouragement, a high-five or a hug. His colleagues are exactly the same, never missing an opportunity to smile or to say a positive word to one another. This isn't something you can fake: it comes from a deep place of caring and a knowledge that we all achieve more when we work together.

'Nobody misses a Friday' because it is a day when the school comes together in a deep and meaningful way, and it's not all about Chris. What is so impressive about these assemblies is the level of involvement of the children. Children help to run the show, meaning that they feel valued as true partners in the school's success.

In an authentic school community, *everyone* feels as though they play a part.

> *I can't do my job without my brilliant teachers, my brilliant teaching assistants, my brilliant senior leaders . . . they follow the dream.*

Many schools claim to have values such as 'teamwork', 'kindness' or 'respect', but how many of them truly live these values in the way that they operate? It is extremely easy to *say* that you value these things, but how does it look when lived and breathed by everybody?

Because Chris is such a charismatic person, you can be fooled into assuming that the school will all be about him. This couldn't be further from the truth. Chris is all about others: his team, the children and the parents. Yes, Chris might be the one who fires everybody up and he might be the one who paints the visionary picture of the school's future success, but ultimately, he understands that to execute the dream you need everyone on board and playing their part. He has worked hard to build his colleagues' confidence and to raise their aspirations for what might be possible in future.

Chris wants every member of his school community to feel as if they belong and to know that they each have something to offer. He realises that personal growth only comes when you let people try, and that will sometimes mean failing, too. How many headteachers would confidently allow their students (including individuals who have been excluded from other settings) to take visitors around their school all day, unmonitored? How many heads would have so much trust in their staff that they'd happily tell a visitor to go wherever they want in the school and to talk to whoever they like? This is a sign of a powerful and united school community; somewhere where the Head truly trusts his staff and pupils. Chris has complete confidence that they will do themselves – and him – proud.

> *It is the best job in the world, changing people's lives and giving people opportunities.*

As with any team, you must establish a common purpose: something you're all working towards together. Without this vision, staff can feel as if they're sailing on a rudderless ship. At Parklands, the dream is simple: they want to drastically improve the life chances of the children in their care. In a job that can be so exhausting at times, having a 'big picture' of what you're aiming for can be extremely energising and can help to unite all stakeholders around this shared vision.

For Chris, his vision is only able to materialise if everyone contributes. If you visit the Parklands website, you'll see that this is the first thing that is spoken about within their 'ethos' section:

Contribute

- To be an inclusive school where everyone can contribute.
- To ensure that all children are given equal opportunities.
- To enable parents, carers and the wider community to be partners in the aims of the school.

The third point here is easy to overlook. Chris is keen to ensure that members of the wider community also feel like partners in the dream. During the Friday assemblies, parents attend in large numbers and feel part of the celebration. Chris and his staff work relentlessly to engage with parents and show them the same warmth and kindness that they direct towards their pupils. Chris also has incredible links with many local businesses that he invites in and 'sells the dream' to. Because of this, Chris receives incredible investment from these businesses because they want to be part of the magic that is Parklands.

> It just shows that with a dream, high expectations, belief, leading through love (not through a stick), these children can achieve absolutely anything.

Most teachers who persevere with a career in teaching do so because they experience great satisfaction in making a difference to young people's lives. The fact that you have picked up this book suggests that you are one of those people. It's humbling to be reminded, however, that we make no difference at all on our own. We are each a single cog in an enormous machine.

If you think back to anything good or worthwhile you have achieved as a teacher, it's unlikely you did it all by yourself. Perhaps you've had an incredible partnership with a Teaching Assistant who supported you on those dark days when you felt like giving up. Perhaps if you're a leader, you'll be able to recall initiatives you've successfully implemented with the help of some amazing colleagues. Even if you're a solo class teacher, with no TA at all, you'll know that you depend on the children in your classroom to work as a team so that all individuals are able to flourish and make progress.

In an increasingly individualistic society, let's use Chris Dyson's story as an inspiration and as a timely reminder of what can be achieved when we work collectively. Let's be lifted by his message that the 'stick' is not needed as a means to energise or influence others. What might we achieve if we all commit to working more coherently together? How many more young people's lives could we improve if we were to fully recognise the part that we *all* play in our schools' successes?

RUSSELL'S REFLECTION

When I became a Deputy Head in 2018, I was very excited about the prospect of having a greater influence over whole-school culture and the chance to influence teaching practice in every year group. But, in equal measure, I was also feeling deeply disheartened by what I'd experienced in the years before. At every school I'd worked in, I'd watched great teachers and leaders slowly becoming crippled by insecurity and worry about the impact of accountability measures. I was really starting to wonder whether schools could be 'successful' (in terms of good academic results and decent Ofsted grades) while also being pleasant places to work. This visit to Parklands was a golden opportunity to see whether the type of school culture that I dreamt of could truly work in practice. In this reflection, I want to focus on some of the ways that the visit affected my leadership when I returned to my school in Exeter. Whatever your role happens to be, I hope these points will resonate with you – I think they apply to everyone.

There's no doubt that the visit affected my perception of my colleagues. I've always felt as though I valued those around me, and I definitely consider myself a 'people person'. But as anyone who works in a school knows, we're often so busy cracking on with our own personal workload that we can forget to take the time to acknowledge those around us and the contribution they make. When I returned from Parklands, I found that I started seeing my colleagues with fresh eyes. I experienced a renewed appreciation for the part that everybody played in making my school a beautiful place to be. This included colleagues in every role imaginable, and those we can often overlook, such as our caretakers, cleaning teams or the office staff. Since my visit, I think I have made more time to talk to my colleagues and to remember to say 'thank you', particularly for those little (but significant) things that people do for the school. I now find that when I'm recruiting for a new member of staff and I take them on a tour of the school, I closely observe who the candidate says 'hello' to. For example, do they address the teachers but ignore the cleaner who smiles at them? In my eyes, none of us is more important than anybody else.

Taking this point about relationships a little further, my next reflection is about the invisible 'front' that I and many other educators are sometimes guilty of putting up. It's not to say that this is a conscious thing, and perhaps we sometimes do it as a self-protection strategy. For example, maybe leaders sometimes avoid showing too much warmth in case it is perceived as a weakness. After visiting Parklands, though, I realised (in a very profound way) that a big part of great leadership is about being truly honest with yourself and the things that matter to you. Chris Dyson is the same 'Chris' whether he is sitting having a cup of tea with a parent or supporting a vulnerable child in a corridor. His leadership is successful because he knows what matters to him and he's not afraid to be himself. I found this incredibly uplifting and vowed to be more honestly 'me' in my school. What this meant was that

I became less anxious about colleagues seeing all sides of me. It meant that I connected more instantly with parents because I met them where they were and didn't overthink my interactions. In a powerful school community, everyone needs to be themselves, and it is this authenticity that builds trust.

Another instant change upon my return to Exeter was our daily assemblies. Alongside my Headteacher, we put together a new weekly timetable for assemblies (some that were inspired by Parklands and some that were based on our own passions). Now, in a usual week, we have a very values-driven story assembly, spelling bees, times-table competitions, singing and celebration assemblies. We didn't try to clone Chris's assemblies – it would be disingenuous to do so. We simply recognised that coming together as a whole school (or in key stages) was a golden opportunity to make our children feel amazing and as though they belonged to something bigger than themselves. In the podcast, Chris talks about leaders driving the things they are passionate about and letting those beautiful seeds grow. Like Chris, I'm 'maths mad' and introduced a times-table assembly that I deliver in my own way. This is now my favourite time of the week. I see my Tuesday assemblies as a wonderful chance to connect with hundreds of children, to make them feel special and to energise the school community.

An interesting result of the visit was how I came to understand the powerful link between vision (or the 'dream', as Chris calls it) and a united school community. When we are woolly in our thinking, this ripples out negatively to those around us. This is the case if you are a leader trying to run a school, but also if you are a teacher trying to deliver a lesson. When we lack clarity in our purpose, it's demotivating for ourselves and everyone around us. On the contrary, educators who have clarity of vision inevitably enliven and draw in those around them. Think of your most effective lessons – I can imagine there was a precision in your thinking about what you wanted to achieve. The children sensed that clarity of purpose and came on board with you. And so is the case with leadership. The visit to Parklands helped to crystallise our vision for what our school could be. In leadership, when your vision becomes clearer, those around you who like this vision are drawn in further and energised by the big picture you portray to them. But it might also be the case that some colleagues decide that the school is *not* heading in a direction that suits them and they choose to move on. This happened in our case and it was all part of the healthy evolution of our school.

I will forever be grateful for being able to visit Parklands and meet Chris. It gave me a profound sense of how belonging and community underpin everything that we do. It made me realise that great schools can (and should) be built on a foundation of nurture and respect.

STEVE'S REFLECTION

While sadly I didn't attend Parklands Primary School with Russell, the great thing about listening to a podcast is the ability to feel transported and as if you're suddenly part of the conversation you're listening to. When listening to Russell's interview, I strongly sensed Chris's passion and love for his school. This fired me up to implement many of my own ideas within my school community.

When I was looking for my first teaching role, I was overjoyed to find a position advertised for a new community primary school right in the centre of a brand-new housing development. The school had a clear aim: to be a real 'community hub' that brought local people together. Perfect! My Head at the time was deeply passionate about this concept and believed in the philosophy that it takes a whole community to raise every child. I loved this concept (rooted in the African philosophy *ubuntu*, meaning 'humanity'), and this has stuck with me as I have moved through different leadership roles at the school. A deep sense of togetherness is most certainly a key ingredient in the success of any school and something I work hard to achieve as both teacher and leader.

As Russell has focused more on the wider school community, I would like to focus my reflection on the sense of community that we can achieve in our individual classrooms. I have always loved being a class teacher (aside from some occasional pointless paperwork tasks) and I will always love it for one simple reason: the children. How privileged we are to be working daily with little people who can inspire us as much as we inspire them. As Chris rightly says in the podcast, it is the best job in the world as we are changing children's lives and giving them new opportunities. It is for this reason that I have always treated my classes as my extended family. I think that every teacher reading this will know what I mean when I say that sometimes your own family wonders if you give more time to your class than to them. Clearly, this shouldn't be the case and we must establish a healthy work–life balance. But I believe that it is vitally important that we build loving, caring and nurturing bonds with our classes and facilitate this between the children, too. I really do believe that children will work harder when they respect you and each other. In a beautiful class community, we all know that we're cared for and that we have each other's interests at heart.

So what can we do in our classrooms to foster this sense of community? If you are a primary school teacher you might teach around thirty pupils with different passions, backgrounds, strengths and challenges. It is my view that these differences should be celebrated at every opportunity. There are simple ways we can do this, such as showing a genuine interest in the diverse religions within the class during RE lessons or celebrating the successes of students who have done something special outside of school (such as achieving in a sports event). When children see that these little things about each other really matter, we develop empathy, understanding and respect.

Modelling respectful interactions is also vital. I work hard as a teacher to demonstrate a respectful demeanour with every student. When children see this regularly they're more likely to reciprocate and also show this to each other. Building on these positive communications, we strive for success collectively. I see my class as my 'school family' and I want my pupils to see that we achieve incredible things when we work together. This passion for 'being the best that we can be' means we take great pride when winning 'class of the week', having as many 'top readers' as possible or putting on show-stopping assemblies. Being proud of ourselves is important to me: we shine as a collective and we show how amazing we are when we come together. There are also simple shifts in our language that can support this culture, such as using pronouns like 'us', 'we' and 'ours' at every opportunity to show that we are not isolated individuals focused solely on our own goals.

A positive class community means having the highest expectations for every child in the class. After all, we only succeed if we all succeed. Yes, the 'level of success' might look different for individual students, but we must have a mentality of supporting everyone to achieve. This is something that resonated with me from the podcast. Chris clearly appreciates all the children in his school and Parklands is a truly inclusive environment where everyone can be the best that they can be.

It is important to note that developing a strong sense of community in the classroom takes time and certainly a lot of effort. A true class community is the result of thousands of positive interactions and the more children see your nurturing approach, the more it will snowball and transform the class culture. Speak to any teacher who has their own class and they will talk about the amazing feeling a few months into the year when they've got the class where they want them, with children working more as a coherent unit.

Working at Parklands sounds like an absolute dream. Chris certainly inspired me, and what he has achieved in that community is to be admired. I encourage everyone reading this to really cherish the bonds they have in their school, for these relationships are the foundations of all success.

YOUR REFLECTION

Take some time to digest what you've read during this chapter. We have provided some question prompts that you may like to consider, depending on your current role or level of experience.

Support staff

- In your classroom, children will realise that 'community' is important when the adults show them that it is. Could you go out of your way to praise children who focus as much on helping others as they do on themselves?
- Do you have any particular hobbies or interests that you could offer your school, perhaps in the form of a lunchtime club? Often, creating these spaces can make children feel as if they belong to something special – beyond their own class communities.
- What opportunities do you have each day to communicate with parents? You play a vital part in bridging that gap between home and school, and any words of kindness, reassurance or smiles will help to build trust between home and school.

Trainee teachers

- During your placements in different schools, observe how close-knit the different school communities seem to be. Why do you think that some of the schools seem to be happier and friendlier places? How do staff interact with one another in the happier schools, and how can you take this forward into your first teaching role?
- When teaching, are you going out of your way to model the kind of caring and considerate interactions you want to see the children showing each other? Remember that your tone ultimately sets the culture for how the children will treat one another.

- When visiting prospective schools, look at how the staff and children interact. Is the headteacher happy to see their colleagues? Are you welcomed warmly? These can be good indicators of the kind of school community you're considering joining.

Teachers

- Children will often demonstrate the behaviours that we choose to notice. Could you challenge yourself in the weeks ahead to actively acknowledge the behaviours you see that support the development of a more positive class community?
- Considering Russell's point about vision, are you always clear enough with the children about what you're aiming for and why? Remember that clarity of vision draws the team towards a common goal.
- If you are lucky enough to have a Teaching Assistant, the dynamic between the two of you is an important model for children. Do you go out of your way to publicly acknowledge and appreciate your TA? Not only will they feel brilliant, but children will see that this kind of interaction is the 'norm' in the class community.

Senior leaders

- As a leader, you set the tone for how staff and children will treat others, and colleagues will pay close attention to the things that you choose to notice. Are you equitable in your recognition of different colleagues' contributions, regardless of their roles in the school? Do staff receive more praise and recognition than they do niggly reminders?
- Considering your assembly times, is there anything you can tweak to make this more of a bonding experience for the school community? When leading assemblies, could you be more intentional in using collective language ('family', 'team', etc.)? Could your assemblies involve greater participation from children?
- Do parents and carers ever have the opportunity to contribute to your school's vision? How could you reach out to your parent community and see what they are able to offer? This also goes for local businesses. Are there any big companies working nearby who you could invite in to support you or to help with the delivery of an aspect of the curriculum?

CHAPTER 3

WELLBEING

LINKED PODCAST EPISODES:
Wellbeing with Stu Newberry and Wellbeing webinar episodes

GUESTS:
Liz Scott and Stu Newberry

IN THIS CHAPTER WE EXPLORE:

- an alternative way of looking at wellbeing;
- the implications of running our schools with wellbeing as the foundation;
- how we might respond to children and colleagues who are in distress.

ABOUT US: LIZ SCOTT AND STU NEWBERRY

We have been professional listeners/coaches and trainers for over ten years, but before this we each had careers in different professions. Stuart worked in the Police (he retired as a Detective Superintendent) and Liz worked for the BBC as a radio reporter. Over the years, we have explored dozens of psychological concepts and trainings. However, the most meaningful and significant was the 'inside-out' understanding. This is something that now underpins all the work we do in schools, businesses and the wider community.

We are a husband-and-wife team working at the heart of communities through our Social Enterprise 'Inner Compass Guide CIC'. Our work in schools focuses on a simple understanding around the true source of wellbeing. For us, wellbeing isn't something to do or to obtain. We show teachers, leaders and students that wellbeing is at the essence of each and every person.

Many people in school communities experience mental exhaustion. The workload and pace of life leads many to experience anxiety, stress and worry. The message of the Inner Compass Guide is simple: people are pointed back to their internal guidance system – an 'inner compass' that brings their minds back into balance. This inner compass is natural and inbuilt into everyone's psychological system. When people understand how mood, thoughts and beliefs can cloud over their wellbeing (but can never damage it), then they start to experience a sense of ease, freedom and relief. When people realise how their inner compass will always point them back to wellbeing, they start to take notice of it more readily.

This message of wellbeing is proving inspirational in our local community of Ivybridge in Devon. We have been training up community 'Wellbeing Listeners' within charities, health services, businesses and services. This collaborative approach of bringing together key clubs and groups to share conversations around wellbeing is rippling out across the town. Our aspiration is to bring together community groups, families, businesses and schools. As people start to learn about the true nature of inbuilt wellbeing, this will lead to thriving relationships and nourishing interactions across the whole community.

LIZ SCOTT AND STU NEWBERRY: THE INTERVIEWS

When Russell relocated to Devon in 2015, Liz Scott and Stu Newberry were brought in to coach a newly established Senior Leadership team, of which Russell was a part. It didn't take long for Russell and his colleagues to realise that Liz and Stu had a very different take on wellbeing from what they had previously encountered. Liz and Stu focus their work on what can be termed an 'inside-out' understanding of wellbeing. Key to this are some basic principles:

- 100 per cent of our experience is generated through the lens of our thinking. This is why the same situation can look and feel completely different on two separate occasions.
- Wellbeing isn't something we 'achieve' through activity; it's innate: at the core of who we are; we're solid, resilient and wise.
- Our moods shouldn't be conflated with wellbeing. Moods come and go, whereas wellbeing is about a deeper sense of peace, resilience and calm. This 'part of us' is constant, unlike the fleeting nature of moods and feelings.

Over the course of a few years, this understanding would prove to have a transformative and life-changing effect on Russell.

When the podcast was launched in 2018, Russell was keen to record an episode with Stu Newberry. For Steve, this would be his first experience talking to Stu and a chance to hear more about this way of looking at wellbeing. Wellbeing would often arise as a strand in subsequent episodes, but fast-forward another year, and we were all hit with a rather unexpected sledgehammer: the Coronavirus pandemic. During this difficult time, we were keen to provide an offer of support to teachers, so we recorded a series of live 'wellbeing webinars' with both Liz and Stu, exploring a range of themes, including anxiety, dealing with speculation and supporting colleagues who were struggling. This chapter is inspired by both the original interview with Stu and the webinars we went on to record a year later.

> You're in an outcomes-driven occupation and it looks like your wellbeing is attached to outcomes. So, in other words: 'I'll be OK if we get a good Ofsted report' or 'We'll be OK if our children give us good SATs results'.

Having worked extensively with leaders and teachers, Liz and Stu know the pressure that educators often feel. They've watched several leaders leave the profession through stress and they've coached numerous teachers who spend their lives in 'revved-up' thinking. In the quotation above, Stu is pointing to something very common in our schools: a feeling that our wellbeing is dependent on outcomes. It is something that we have experienced, too, both as class teachers trying to ensure great progress for our children and then as a leaders working to improve whole-school outcomes. It can certainly feel as though wellbeing is something you can only get a grip on once your Ofsted grading is positive and when your results end up looking strong. But what are the implications of operating our schools with this belief? How might it affect the environments we create for young people to learn in?

What's happened as a human race is we've got so busy in our thinking, scrambling around trying to find wellbeing – anywhere other than in ourselves – that this can be a very mentally exhausting process.

Liz and Stu would suggest that the fundamental problem with wellbeing is that many people don't really understand how our psychological system works. As a result, we search for wellbeing in the wrong places: good SATs results or a positive lesson observation, for example. It's great that the education system has recognised that there is a toxic issue with stress, but unfortunately because wellbeing is so often seen as something we need to 'go and get' we've seen tokenistic responses from many leaders. Compulsory yoga is the classic well-meaning but misguided example of this.

In one of our wellbeing webinars, Liz was reflecting on this issue even further. In the midst of a terribly challenging time, she was encouraging our listeners to look inwards rather than outwards for feelings of wellbeing. She made the point that it is perfectly natural to experience low moods and worked-up thinking when times are tricky, but that the real distress we often experience is not because of the 'thing' that is happening around us, but the layers of overthinking we innocently pile on top of our initial thought. We've become accustomed to responding to stressful thoughts by getting more busy and more stressed trying to solve what we believe to be the problem. In reality, the main causes of our distress are not what we'd like to believe – Ofsted or a pandemic – but overthinking. We particularly like the analogy of the snow-globe for this. When we're distressed, it's as if our mind is a furiously shaken-up snow-globe. In our desire to fix our stories, we innocently shake it up some more and then wonder why we're still not feeling any better. Liz and Stu say that, as humans, we have an incredible psychological system that recalibrates when we slow down and lets our thinking settle. When we stop shaking the snow-globe, we get clarity. From that place of clarity, we are then able to judge what to do next. Now, just imagine if every teacher and leader you ever worked with understood this simple concept. How many ridiculous emails would remain unsent? How many interactions would be more understanding rather than passive–aggressive? How many more great decisions for children would be made?

When wellbeing is at the heart of an organisation and you create the right environment, then the chances are that the results will look after themselves.

Wellbeing is not a consequence of good outcomes; it should be the foundation of them. Unfortunately, in the education system we find ourselves in, many of us have been suckers for the narrative that wellbeing and good outcomes are incompatible. Too many leaders sadly believe that they need to put immense pressure on themselves and their teams in order to achieve the outcomes they are so desperate for. Thinking back to the previous chapter, Chris Dyson demonstrated in his school that a foundation of love and nurture *could* allow every teacher and child to be at their best. In his school, great results and an 'outstanding' grading were the by-product of a beautiful working environment.

Imagine a school where both adults and children arrive each day feeling positive, valued and keen to do their best. Wanting great outcomes for children is certainly important, but surely the right way to achieve them is by creating workplaces and classrooms where everyone can thrive?

> *Fundamentally, at the core of who you truly are, you are perfect. You are whole and perfect. That applies to you as teachers and leaders in education, and it also applies to the children that you teach.*

The inside-out understanding of wellbeing has massive implications. It makes the case that humans already have everything they need to navigate through life. Yes, there will be dramatic ups and downs – this is an inevitable part of the human experience. Life will be hard; times will test us and very often things won't go the way we expect them to. But Liz and Stu believe that we need to start trusting ourselves more and knowing – in a deep way – that we've got this, and that we can handle the rollercoaster of life. Life seems less frightening when we realise that we can cope with anything that comes our way.

A key bit of the quotation above is that this idea also applies to the young people we work with. Often when we see the tough stuff our students are going through, and when we observe their distressed behaviours, it's all too easy to think that there is something we need to 'fix' or 'sort out' about the child in front of us. Stu is saying here – and this is a huge claim – that our children, just like us, are fundamentally solid at their core. If this is true, how might this change the way we interact with them and support them to handle the circumstances they'll come up against in their lives?

> *There's a perception that young people can push our buttons, but that's just not possible. It looks like that young person is causing me to feel angry, for example. When we get to know how the system works, then we'll see that, innocently, I'm generating my own anger. When we get to see that, the way that we interact with the child is going to be from a place of understanding, rather than a place of anger and annoyance.*

As we navigate through life, we're experiencing every moment through the lens of our thinking. Your thoughts are rather like the 'audio-description feature' you can turn on for films: a voice that talks you through the action. The issue with our internal voice is that it can be wholly unreliable. When we're tired, for example, a simple 'Hello' from a colleague could be perceived negatively, yet we know deep down this is ridiculous. And it's the same with the children we teach. They sometimes navigate through life's challenges with ease, while on other days they implode (or explode) because of overwhelming thinking. You may have noticed that on a good day (for you), when your thinking isn't agitated, you feel as if you can handle anything the children you teach do or say. A child might say something quite rude and you just seem to respond from a place of calm confidence, rather than being drawn into a battle. Yet on a bad day, a pupil might behave in an unacceptable way and you perceive this as a personal vendetta and react accordingly, perhaps escalating the situation further.

It's good to be reminded that young people, just like us, get lost in their thinking sometimes. They, too, make up their own narratives about life, people and circumstances. When they are in overwhelmed thinking, they will muck up. They will let themselves down. They'll act out of line. We have an incredible opportunity when working with young people to help them to understand the nature of their own thinking. By having discussions about this with children, we can help them to see that they don't have to treat their thoughts and feelings as gospel. However, when we try to fix their thinking, or try to persuade them not to feel a certain way, we can inadvertently whip them up further. If we can meet children from our own grounded place of wellbeing, secure in the knowledge that our feelings are transient, then we can help them to embrace the natural ebb and flow of life and navigate through with much greater ease.

RUSSELL'S REFLECTION

When I moved to Devon, something frightening surfaced for me – anxiety. On reflection, I think I'd been walking around with high levels of anxious thinking for many years and the move just exacerbated what was already there beneath the surface.

The relocation to Devon was a dream come true. We'd discussed it for years: a chance to live in our favourite part of the country, a new dream-job for me and an opportunity to raise our children somewhere truly beautiful. Yet when the dream materialised, I experienced internal turmoil. I couldn't get over all the things I felt I was leaving. I came to resent the move. I didn't feel quite right. I walked around with a knot in my stomach – an agitated feeling of being on edge all the time. This came to manifest itself in crippling anxiety attacks, seemingly at the most absurd times. One night it happened while I was trying to get my girls to bed. I had to leave the room because I felt so overwhelmed. My wife came into our bedroom to find me lying on our bed in complete, silent meltdown, with me eventually telling her, 'I feel like I want to die'. On another occasion we had taken our children to the circus – the circus quite literally being the personification of joy and laughter – yet I had to escape the tent because I was falling apart inside and felt that I couldn't breathe.

When Stu started coaching me and talked about the inside-out understanding, I wasn't immediately sold. The most uncomfortable bit was the idea that I was generating my own experiences. I felt quite affronted that I might be innocently engineering my own feelings of distress. Over time, however, I really came to understand the truth in this. I would catch myself spiralling into negative thinking and say to myself, 'Don't take the bait, Russell'. It was as though Stu had helped me to develop a healthy dose of self-awareness. This didn't stop me experiencing anxious thinking or low moods, but it did prevent me from indulging my own narratives and plummeting into overwhelm on a regular basis. I came to realise that a lot of the stories I told myself about the world around me weren't accurate portrayals of my life: they were simply stories I was making up when I was experiencing distressed thinking. I realised that I had been playing my own game of confirmation bias: looking for the evidence to support my view that life was being unfair. Noticing this was the first (massive) step towards a much more fulfilling life.

As time has gone on, my understanding of wellbeing has really deepened. I still go up and down, just like everybody else, but I rarely spiral out of control, and I haven't had a single panic attack in the past five years. I really understand now that, at my core, I'm solid. I know that there is a deeper part of me that is wise and resilient. I think of it as a calm place internally and the beauty is that I can access this at any time I need to. I have learnt not to take the bait of my thinking and I now tend to interpret my low moods as a sign that I probably need a bit of a break or an early night.

How has this understanding impacted my work as an educator? As a leader, I think I make much better decisions than I used to. This manifests itself in all sorts of situations, but most obviously in my relationships with others (the most important part of my job as a Deputy Head). On a typical day I might interact with a highly stressed colleague, an angry parent and a child who is emotionally dysregulated. I know, now, that my best offer to all these people is to meet them with my own sea of calm. I will not be of any service to others if I am in my own worked-up thinking. Instead, from a place of settled thinking I just *know* what to do or find the right words to say. For this reason, I'm not that keen on tools and techniques for leadership – these approaches wouldn't help me to interpret the complexity of other human beings in the way that my own inner compass does.

I believe that, as adults in a school, having a firm grasp of wellbeing is the greatest thing we can do for the young people in our care. They deserve to encounter adults who are calm, content and well. Sadly, in my career I've often witnessed the martyrdom that we've all been guilty of: work every hour of the day and then wear our exhaustion like a badge of honour, a sign of how hard we've been working. For me, this is a wholly unhelpful culture for children to be immersed in. Instead, when the adults in the building care about their own wellbeing and operate from a place of calm, great things happen. Beautiful relationships are fostered, kindness becomes the predominant language and wisdom underpins decision-making.

In my school, we've worked hard to develop emotional literacy with our children so they can understand the principles of inside out in their own way. For example, we use a nice little metaphor of red/green glasses. We say that some days, when we're feeling down, it's as if we're wearing red glasses. Through 'red thinking', everything seems scarier and more frightening. On other days, it's as if we're wearing green specs, with life looking more positive and easier to handle. At the start of each school year, we also do a five-point scale activity (quite commonly used as a SEND strategy). We talk about how our bodies let us know that we're feeling stressed and we talk about the things that might help us when we start to feel a certain way. I truly believe that developing self-understanding among young people is one of the greatest gifts we can give them to enable them to live positive, enriching lives.

STEVE'S REFLECTION

I have to be honest from the outset: when I first encountered the buzzword 'wellbeing', I was someone who perceived it with some degree of negativity. In my eyes, it would be a thing that would come and go pretty quickly within the education world. To me, it seemed like a pointless idea, as there was no time to do the day job without having to think also about my wellbeing, as well as that of others. To me, the whole thing seemed tokenistic and all about making leadership feel good about themselves for saying that they cared about our wellbeing. I didn't need my leaders to put on 'Work-out Wednesdays' or place 'healthy life-style' books in the staffroom – great, that would solve all our issues! But then I met Liz and Stu, and wow – my perception changed very quickly.

There's no doubt that wellbeing *can* be tokenistic and an added pressure, but only when it is given this meaningless value. If you want to go ahead and run a yoga session that all staff must attend or hold a chilled-out staff meeting that still forces staff to stay until 5pm, then fair enough, but please know that this is not developing wellbeing – it does quite the opposite. What my conversations with Liz and Stu taught me were that there was a lot more to wellbeing, and the conversation regarding the inside-out understanding went on to really transform my outlook. To go from believing that my wellbeing *was* determined by my class's performance, the SATs results and ultimately an Ofsted inspection, to now understanding that we don't 'achieve' wellbeing this way was so powerful. I am the first to admit that I have been a results-driven person all my life: from the days as a young footballer when I would analyse my weekly performances on a chart in my bedroom, to being a solicitor where case-success percentages were there to be celebrated, to being a teacher wanting to achieve the best SATs results. Sure, it is fine to want to achieve the best as a teacher, and I always want the children in our school to be the very best they can be, but to think that my wellbeing depended on this stuff just couldn't be right. This simply isn't what wellbeing is.

With my eyes open to the idea that wellbeing is innate, and beginning to look from the inside out, I started to understand more about myself and my moods in general. I sometimes wake up and feel in a bad mood for no reason. I go to bed happy, I sleep well and for some reason I don't feel right when I wake up. I've learnt that this is all part of the human experience and not something I need to overthink or worry about.

Importantly, I also began to be more aware of the wellbeing of others around me. Being a leader, I have always invested time in the wellbeing of staff, children and other stakeholders. This was true when working as a criminal and family solicitor – I always wanted to help those who were struggling. But what Stu and Liz opened my eyes to was the idea that those around me don't need fixing. My job is to be a person that people can relate to, and my kindest offer is often just to provide that listening ear. It isn't useful for me to get worked up when a member of staff acts a little sharply in the staffroom; it isn't helpful for me to be defensive when an angry parent challenges a school decision, and it isn't productive to let a child 'get under my skin' when they are having a particularly bad day.

What benefits those around me is being grounded in my own wellbeing. It provides a foundation for kindness and compassion, and enables clarity to flow as a result. This helps me as a school leader to provide a calm, loving and positive environment for our children to attend school. It also creates a culture where staff know they have people on hand to support them when life throws one of its tricky curve balls at them. The same goes for our children, too. Like Russell, my school uses the five-point scale to discuss emotions, and to know that it is OK to feel sad or angry. We know that feelings are perfectly normal, and adults won't panic and try to fix children's emotions by slapping a 'plaster' on things when children wobble.

Wellbeing is much deeper than I initially realised. The more we can fully understand wellbeing, the more it will provide the secure foundations to build schools where children and adults all thrive. As Jaz Ampaw-Farr said in Chapter 1, we are all 'everyday heroes', but in order to be these heroes for the young people in our care, we're stronger when we are grounded in the knowledge that, at our core, we're all OK.

YOUR REFLECTION

Take some time to digest what you've read during this chapter. We have provided some question prompts that you may like to consider, depending on your current role or level of experience.

Support staff

- In this chapter, we thought about the importance of being grounded in our own wellbeing. What makes the 'snow-globe' of your mind settle?
- Are you ever guilty of trying to 'fix' how a young person feels? How about trying to listen and reassure, rather than getting lost in the stories your pupils tell you when they're upset?
- Your partnership with teachers is so much more powerful when underpinned by this understanding of wellbeing. Sometimes your teacher might need you to notice the resilience and strength you see in them. How might you point this out to them in the days or weeks ahead?

Trainee teachers

- During your training, you have a great opportunity to observe school staff in the settings where you carry out your placements. Can you tell which adults are grounded in their wellbeing, or indeed not? What effect does this have on their interactions with others?
- You might find that as you take on more teaching responsibility, anxious thinking can affect the way you interact with young people. What impact might it have on your interactions to realise that a young person can't ever 'push your buttons' or 'make you' feel anxious?
- Have a go at responding from your own 'sea of calm' next time you notice a student in worked-up thinking. How do they respond when you listen from a place of compassion, rather than trying to fix their feelings?

Teachers

- Here's a challenge: in the week ahead, try to notice yourself spiralling into overthinking. What difference does it make when you spot yourself doing this, rather than getting lost in the stories?
- In your class, there may well be a child or two who you've fallen into a bit of a negative rut with. Perhaps you've taken the bait of your thinking and decided they 'push your buttons'. How might this relationship look from a place of settled thinking? How might you see them differently?
- We all feed off each other's moods. When you notice a colleague getting wound up about something, what is your greatest offer? What happens when – instead of indulging their stories and getting wound up yourself – you meet them with your own 'sea of calm'?

Senior leaders

- The phone rings: it's a parent wanting to talk to you. A story we might often tell ourselves at this point is, 'Oh, no! Here we go!' But what if you remind yourself at this point that at your core, you're solid and that you can handle anything? How might that change the way the conversation goes?
- You can send the most incredible ripple effects through your school. If you spent a little more time this week on yourself, how might that affect the kind of ripples you generate?
- Your time and energy are precious. When you see that it's your job to fix others' feelings and problems, you exhaust yourself in the process. If you were to spend more time calmly listening this week and less time solving, how might that shift the dynamic in your school?

CHAPTER 4

INCLUSIVE PRACTICE

LINkED PODCAST EPISODE:
Inclusive Practice with Gareth Morewood

GUEST:
Gareth Morewood

> **IN THIS CHAPTER WE EXPLORE:**
>
> - how to create a culture where inclusive practice is the norm;
> - inclusive practices that benefit everybody;
> - the importance of anticipating the stressors some children will experience and working with individuals to respond to these constructively;
> - the power of inclusive curricula.

ABOUT ME: GARETH MOREWOOD

I am currently the Educational Advisor for Studio III (www.studio3.org), previously having worked for 25 years in UK schools, the last 17 of which were as SENCo (Special Educational Needs Coordinator) in a large inclusive secondary school in the northwest of England.

I have been very fortunate not only with my substantive roles, but also in gaining extensive 'front-line' experience supporting schools, families and working directly with young people in the UK and abroad, most recently in Chile, Dubai, Portugal, Scandinavia and Ireland.

Previously, as an Honorary Research Fellow at the University of Manchester, I worked on a range of projects, predominantly regarding the inclusion of young people with complex needs and in supporting autistic learners in their local schools as part of the wider inclusion agenda. Currently as a Visiting Lecturer at the University of Chester, I lead on postgraduate modules relating to the provision for complex needs as part of the wider inclusive agenda.

With my work at Studio III, I am Co-Director of the LASER Programme, which fuses my critically acclaimed Saturation Model (Morewood et al., 2011) with Low Arousal approaches (McDonnell and Deveau, 2018) as part of a system-led model of inclusive practice. The first LASER courses ran during 2020.

I have written and recorded a significant body of published works, films and resources about being inclusive as a school, setting and community. I continue to strive for every young person, whatever their starting point or background, to have the necessary understanding, support and provision to ensure that they achieve their best potential.

Hopefully, this chapter gives a flavour of some of the things I have been involved with and also the ideas I continue to have and develop looking forward.

GARETH MOREWOOD: THE INTERVIEW

The first time we heard Gareth speak, we knew that we wanted to discuss inclusive practice with him. He has a remarkably down-to-earth demeanour, a clear way of explaining things and his expertise in the field of SEND is extraordinary. In this episode, we covered a lot of ground regarding inclusive practice, looking at the challenges that many young people face in our schools and how we can create classrooms and whole-school environments where every individual can thrive. Gareth helped us to think about the philosophies and beliefs that underpin a lot of our conversations about inclusive practice, as well as the practical things we can do to support all our students to succeed in school.

> *The environments and contexts which we're asking young people to learn in, engage with and understand are very complex.*

We started by reflecting on the challenges facing many young people in schools. Gareth quite rightly pointed out that schools are very complex places. First, there's the physical environment, but within that is the fact that every school has several unique spaces within it: classrooms, corridors, school halls, canteens, playgrounds and so on. Each of these spaces creates a very different sensory experience for children, and they all have the potential to be quite overwhelming. Then, of course, you have the rules and guidelines that accompany each of these spaces. In the podcast, Gareth gave the example of a high school canteen where children have been taught to walk right around the snaking passageway (made by those elasticated things that stretch between metal posts). Children may have been taught not to cut through or across this passageway, yet most children would understand that there may be rare occasions when there might be an exception to this rule – for example, when there are only a handful of people in the canteen. Some of our young people, who may not read these social cues so easily, might find it distressing or confusing to be told that the rule they *normally* have to follow doesn't apply today.

So, a good starting point for strong inclusive practice is simply realising that not every child sees and experiences the world in the same way – everybody is unique. Gareth cited his good friend Ellie Chapple and encouraged us to 'flip the narrative', not trying to make young people fit into a pre-existing system but looking at how we can allow them to be themselves and still thrive. He talked about the simple adjustments that can be made to environments that support children who easily experience sensory overload. For example, by considering the harshness of the lighting in a room or the way that sound reverberates around it, we can make our school buildings more welcoming spaces for *all* children.

Building on this idea of inclusive environments, what about the way that we teach? How can we ensure that all children are able to access their learning and make good progress in our schools?

> *If you think about what's a good strategy for young people who have a diagnosis, additional needs, who've had difficult starts in life, or perhaps were in care, these are good strategies for everybody.*

What we really enjoyed about speaking to Gareth was how he demystified good inclusive teaching. He didn't reel off an enormous list of strategies we need to employ to make our classrooms inclusive, but instead talked about doing more of the simple things that consistently benefit every learner. For example, you might have a child in your class who feels much less anxious when they can see a visual timetable of the day displayed in the classroom. Will other learners be harmed by this? Of course not. In fact, you might have a large proportion of children in your class who find it reassuring to know what is planned, how the time progresses and what to expect. Indeed, this may also apply for other strategies, like providing clear visual cues during lessons for children who find complex verbal instructions difficult to process. We know from cognitive science that the working memory has a limited capacity, so every other child in that classroom will also benefit from some visual reminders about what they need to do. When we do these simple things that particularly benefit certain individuals, we inevitably support all learners to achieve. A key feature of inclusive practice is simply making sure that Quality First Teaching underpins all that we do.

> *Calm, consistent routines are essential.*

A central feature of Gareth's work is helping educators to understand the potential stressors a child might experience during the school day. Transitions would be a classic example of this. He talked about a high school setting where they might choose to swap the noisy bell or alarm between lessons for a calm verbal indication from the teachers that it's time for the lesson to end. By making this simple adjustment, the school creates a calmer climate for all learners while reducing the stress of those who would find the loud noise unbearable. In a primary setting, this might involve having a really effective system for how pupils get changed for PE or line up after break, for example. These 'pinch points' in the day can be really quite distressing for some students, so by thinking more carefully about our systems and processes, we can create a calmer and more inclusive environment for everybody.

Gareth also emphasised the importance of consistency to reduce unnecessary stressors for our pupils. When you think about this, it makes complete sense. Imagine being a child, trying desperately hard to cope within the complex environment of a school. You might encounter dozens of different adults each day. Now imagine how distressing or difficult it must be for some learners when every one of those adults chooses to provide different rules, guidelines or instructions, or perhaps interprets whole-school systems differently. For children who are prone to high levels of anxiety, we inadvertently raise their arousal levels when we allow inconsistency to reign. As teachers, we can avoid this even within our individual classrooms. For a primary school teacher, you might choose to stick to one clear way of asking the children to stop, rather than changing this on a regular basis. You may decide to have clear, consistent boundaries about what you will or won't accept, and these goalposts won't shift on a daily basis depending on your mood. Consistency and calm go hand in hand.

The key is really focusing on the individual. It's not about saying 'that's a 12-year-old with ADHD'. It's about knowing that's Alex, or Ahmed, or Sarah. Everyone's unique.

Gareth reminded us that every child is unique and we must avoid clunky generalisations. We have to be careful when talking about 'what works' for an autistic child or someone with a diagnosis of ADHD, for example, because not every child with these diagnoses is the same. Yes, there are principles of inclusive practice (some we have outlined already) that will benefit everyone, but then there are the incredible relationships that sit on top of this. As teachers, we're in the privileged position of being able to get to know our students really well over time. In some cases, it can take a significant amount of investment to fully appreciate a child's triggers and challenges, but also their amazing gifts and abilities. When trying to create inclusive learning environments, there must be a conscious effort from every adult to get to know the individual children in their care. We won't always get things right, but a key thing is to always remain professionally curious about what is going to work for each child – in essence, being a reflective practitioner.

Speak to the family and the young person. It's about approaching things in a solution-focused way. It's about saying, 'How could we do this?'

Sometimes it can feel rather overwhelming thinking about how best to help a student. If they present behaviours that we haven't seen before, or if they have a bespoke need we have not yet encountered, we can feel intimidated by the prospect of getting it wrong. As a result of that insecurity, it is all too easy to say that we can't help and only see a 'problem'. However, Gareth talked in the episode about the importance of co-production as a way of supporting young people to be successful. It's about having a mentality of 'we can do this together' and listening to the young person and their family – they are the people who know more about their needs than anybody else. It is good to be reminded that there is not a SENDCo or a teacher in the land who has encountered every unique need or who knows what to do in every given situation. A key part of inclusive practice is having an open-minded perspective where you want to learn, where you are keen to try different strategies and where you are ready to listen to the young person in front of you.

If you're stressed as an individual, you're not only going to limit what you're able to do with the young people, but you're highly likely to pass that stress on. The time to plan is when people are calm, not when people are in crisis.

In the previous chapter, we talked about the importance of our own wellbeing and realising how our own calmness is of significant benefit to those around us. This is a key feature of Gareth's work: being self-aware and understanding how our emotional states may affect those we encounter at school. We have all been in those situations when we're perhaps not dealing very well with a child who is dysregulated, and along comes a calm adult who just seems to find the right words to say and we are able to let them take the lead. Equally, we may have all seen the opposite happen. It's not about us having to always feel brilliant, but it's about having the emotional intelligence to recognise our feelings and stressors. From this space, we can avoid allowing our own low moods to negatively affect the way we handle tricky situations.

The final part of the quotation above is also key. Have you ever been in a situation where a dysregulated child is just starting to calm down, and then someone decides to talk to them about the initial incident a little too soon? Before you know it, the child is feeling cross again and we're back to square one. Gareth is encouraging us here to make plans when everybody is calm. This might mean that we're going to have a proper conversation about an incident a little later on when the child is able to listen and engage in a meaningful dialogue. It might also mean that the adult needs to calm down before engaging any further.

> *I'm obsessed with this idea of peer education and how the curriculum represents different disabilities and needs.*

One thing that arose during the conversation with Gareth was the power of the students themselves in creating an inclusive environment. Gareth is deeply passionate about the curriculum helping to educate young people about different needs and disabilities. Sometimes we can be rather shocked when children display prejudice or naivety about people in society who, in some way, seem to be different from them. But how often is this either learnt from other adults, social media or 'playground whispers', or the result of simply not knowing enough? In the absence of understanding, discrimination of some form sadly often fills the void. If we want to create truly inclusive environments for young people, we need to use every opportunity to educate them about difference. When children are given this space to learn and discuss such key issues, they prove time and time again that they are much more capable of embracing equality and diversity than adults often seem to be.

RUSSELL'S REFLECTION

At the start of my teaching career, I thought I was grossly underequipped to support children with additional needs. I didn't feel as though I'd had enough lectures about SEND and I was frightened of doing something wrong. I quickly learnt, however, that while it is important that teachers receive good training, the most vital thing they can do is to remain committed to keep on learning. As Gareth said in the podcast, every child is an individual and it's imperative we make the effort to learn about their unique needs. For this reason, I want to focus my reflection on some of the amazing children I've met over the years.

During a PGCE placement I met the most incredible autistic boy. He lit up the room with his beautiful personality and, with some careful considerations from the adults, he managed really well in the class. One thing he could find tricky, though, was the very start to the day and he would sometimes refuse to come into the class from the corridor cloakroom. I'll never forget how there was one other child in the class who seemed to have an almost magical way with him. Each morning she would wander calmly into the corridor with a smile, say to the boy, 'Come on, you silly sausage' and in an instant, he would take her hand and walk into the class with her. This was my first lesson in the crucial role that other children play in helping to create inclusive environments. This little girl taught me to always remain calm and to invest time in developing trusting relationships.

In my first year of teaching, I taught an autistic girl. At this stage, I had never heard about autistic masking. By this, I mean the coping strategies that autistic children often use to fit into social situations, often leaving them feeling burnt out and emotionally drained. I remember her mother talking to me about how she would go home some evenings and be really distressed after a day in school. In my ignorance, I thought the parent was being overprotective; to me, the girl seemed happy at school. The turning point was during a music lesson. Being a newly qualified teacher, my classroom organisation wasn't great and the lesson was frankly chaotic. The girl's group was working in the corridor and I looked out of my classroom to find her with her fingers in her ears, on the verge of crying. I felt terrible and realised there was a lot more going on for her than I first realised. As Gareth said in the podcast, families know their children best and at that point I realised I needed to do a better job of listening to her mum.

Much later in my career, when I was no longer class-based, I covered for a Year 6 teacher one afternoon. In the class was a girl who required eye-drops throughout the day because of an incredibly rare skin condition (I speak about this in the podcast). An alarm went off and a child told me it was time to administer the drops. I panicked. Nobody had told me how to do this. What if I got it wrong? Thankfully, the child found it highly entertaining guiding me through this process and, despite missing on my first three attempts, we got there in the end. She knew I was trying my best and was more than happy to help me learn. She taught me to stop fearing new scenarios and to simply embrace every new situation as an opportunity to learn.

As my career has continued, I've found myself having a substantial pastoral role. This has often involved mentoring children with mental health challenges, or in a less planned-for way, being called upon to support in situations where children are highly dysregulated. I believe this has become a real strength of mine and something I am very passionate about. I really relate to Gareth's advice about slowing down our movements and being conscious of our own emotional states. I rarely plan for how I am going to deal with a child who is in crisis (mainly because there isn't usually time) but, as we explored in the previous chapter, meeting the child with my own 'sea of calm' is my greatest offer. From this place, we can coregulate and I can support the individual to come through their intense feelings of distress. This is much easier when we have a pre-existing positive relationship. I can think of a few children I have worked with where, over time, we have coproduced plans for what we will do in moments of crisis. We have talked through the strategies we're going to use when we feel a certain way and I can't say how rewarding it is to watch a child execute their plan safely, instead of hurting someone or ripping down a display board.

I know I've reflected on some key individuals here, but I wanted to end my reflection by thinking about our classes as a whole. A few years into teaching, I was given a class and asked to 'sort them out'. Sadly, they'd earnt a reputation in the school for being difficult. The class included numerous individuals with specific needs. I knew that in order to support them all, my emphasis needed to be on creating a safe, calm climate where everyone could feel secure and learn. I focused my energies on developing clear routines, always having high expectations, and I invested lots of time in talking to their parents. I ended up spending two years with that class. I was pretty exhausted at the end of some days, but it was worth it. I wouldn't call them difficult at all. They were the most incredible bunch of kids who simply needed someone to believe in them, to adore them and to provide them with a clear framework for learning. When I gave them that, they gave me so much in return.

STEVE'S REFLECTION

As someone who is passionate about supporting all children (and always have been), I really felt as if I benefited from the podcast and Gareth's sound advice. The conversation came as a fantastic opportunity for me personally, as my school was just going through an SEND review. I needed the headspace and discussion to allow me to rethink what was in place in our setting, and it gave me some clear principles to guide me in my work back at school.

I remember at my first teaching interview when I said that I would like to learn more about how to support all pupils, particularly those with additional needs, as I felt that I had limited knowledge from my PGCE. Once I'd secured my first teaching position, I remember planning extensively that summer, spending hours upon hours designing a 'knock-out' classroom with displays galore – but that was before I received my class list. 'Hmmm,' I remember anxiously thinking. Two children stood out, highlighted red. Panic set in as I read that they both had complex needs (predominantly autism and ADHD) and that they also presented defiant behaviours. One child was joining from another school and there was very limited information, although I vividly remember the brief note, 'table turner and chair thrower'. Now, being a fresh-faced NQT, I tried to research what I could do prior to meeting these children and how I could prepare myself for Day One. The truth is, while I needed some advice to get me going, there was no need for these children to be 'highlighted red' or for me to be so fearful. They were simply children – sweet, lovely children. I remember nodding along when Gareth spoke about knowing every child as an individual because it is all about that. I created amazing bonds with that class and cherished every child for their own uniqueness. The most important thing for these children was that I modelled a calm, caring and loving demeanour. I also needed to know them for who they were, and not just for the behaviours they sometimes presented. They needed me to look beyond the labels and to focus on nurture, consistency and Quality First Teaching.

Another reflection that is pertinent here is how I set up my classroom. I am the first to admit that having a new classroom to decorate and to set up was always a huge buzz for me. I loved spending summer holidays creating a theme for the class, designing wall art, even creating Shrek's swamp or the Gruffalo's woods in my classroom, including tree trunks for seats and bark all over the floor. (Top tip: don't use bark in the classroom as it stinks after a week or so, especially if there is underfloor heating!) Anyway, I let my passion for design dictate the classroom layout rather than considering the needs of the 30 children who would have to use it. I quickly adapted my practice as I became better accustomed to the needs of my classes. Gareth is so right when he discusses the need for a safe, consistent and calming environment where children know the routines and what to expect each day. I remember our leadership team asking every teacher to display a visual timetable, and while some people were sceptical, I remember a quiet girl in my class coming up to me and telling me how she felt better going to school every day as she always worried about what lesson would be in the afternoon. I would not have initially thought that this child would benefit from a visual timetable, but this is what Gareth was saying: inclusive practices will benefit all children.

The idea of using good strategies for all pupils makes me reflect on maths, where we know that manipulatives can really aid conceptual understanding. In my experience, there is still sometimes a perception that only low prior attainers need physical resources, but this can't be right. As the principles of mastery have become more embedded in schools, teachers have seen that the use of physical resources benefits everyone in the classroom to develop a deeper understanding, and not just those who may need a little more time or scaffolding. The same goes for how we select which children a Teaching Assistant might support. In too many lessons I've seen the TA working with a predetermined 'lower' group (we'll explore the problems with this idea more later), but if we really think about quality-first teaching and supporting all children, then surely the children with the most significant needs deserve plenty of access to the person with the most expertise: the teacher?

My final reflection is that every child is a unique individual, and this is a beautiful thing. I have witnessed discussions where someone says they have taught an autistic child before, so they're planning to repeat what worked for that child with the new individual they're about to teach. This simply cannot be right. Students and learners with additional needs share as many differences as they do similarities. Therefore, expecting a single approach or intervention to meet the needs of everyone is naive. What we need to do is avoid generalisations, get to know the children for their amazing selves, build solid foundations for them to achieve and support them in ways that suit them. Stressors will be different for every child, so if we take time to understand these, then we can reduce overwhelming experiences and support everyone to feel safe and secure when in school. This is surely the entitlement of every child.

YOUR REFLECTION

Take some time to digest what you've read during this chapter. We have provided some question prompts that you may like to consider, depending on your current role or level of experience.

Support staff

- Are you expected to support the same groups of children daily? How about talking to your class teacher about this? Would they benefit from more opportunities to work more independently or with the teacher sometimes?
- Remember that unwanted behaviours can be a symptom of a child's anxiety or distress. Can you think of any individuals who it might be worth asking what they're feeling worried about? You might just unlock the real issue.
- Pre-empting stressful scenarios can prevent many issues arising in the first place. Think of a normal school day. Are there certain pinch points where you could do something a little differently to reduce the anxiety levels of an individual or indeed the whole class?

Trainee teachers

- During your placements, you're going to meet a range of unique children. Try to be as professionally curious as you can. After reading this chapter, could you ask the normal class teacher to tell you more about any individuals who you are worried about?
- Think about your routines when teaching. Do you notice any times of the day when children might be more likely to struggle because of how things are set up? Could you make any simple tweaks to make this an easier time for the children to navigate?
- Never underestimate the power of listening to children. If you have any children in your placements who seem to be finding things tricky, have you considered asking them what they're finding hard and how they'd like you to help them?

Teachers

- How could you harness the children in creating a more inclusive environment? Are children encouraged to talk about their experiences of disability or difference, or to share with their peers the things they find tricky? Personal, Social, Health and Economic (PSHE) education is a brilliant mechanism for this kind of conversation.
- Children often thrive when they see that their parents and teachers are on the same page. Is there anything you could do to open up a healthier dialogue with parents of children who might be struggling in school?
- Perceptions are powerful in teaching and children are sponges for our anxieties. Could you become more aware of your own emotional states when teaching? Do you model for the children how to express what you're feeling in a healthy way?

Senior leaders

- Inclusive practice stems from the leadership of an organisation. Are you conscious of the language you use about particular children in front of teachers? If they hear you talk about children as a problem, then that will become the norm among colleagues.
- Calm cultures are created by leaders who are calm. Are you emotionally self-aware with your staff and children? When you're feeling stressed, does this come out via snappy emails or terse responses, or do you model the behaviours you hope to see from them?
- As a leader, you have the opportunity to influence whole-school systems that can make your school much more inclusive. For example, have you agreed with staff the way they do simple things such as lining children up or getting them to stop in a lesson? These simple adjustments have the potential to benefit so many children in your school.

REFERENCES

McDonnell, A. and Deveau R. (2018) Low arousal approaches to manage behaviours of concern. *Learning Disability Practice.* doi: 10.7748/ldp.2018.e1882

Morewood, G. D., Humphrey, N. and Symes, W. (2011) Mainstreaming autism: making it work. *Good Autism Practice Journal*, 62–8, 2 December.

CHAPTER 5

REPRESENTATION

LINKED PODCAST EPISODE:
Representation in Children's Literature

GUESTS:
Jasmine Newton, Doaa Al-Soraimi and Ashley Booth

IN THIS CHAPTER WE EXPLORE:

- why every child deserves to see themselves represented in the curriculum;
- the power of stories as mechanisms for representation;
- the importance of representation in helping children to understand perspectives that are different from theirs;
- how effective representation nurtures empathy and understanding in young people.

ABOUT ME: JASMINE NEWTON

My name is Jasmine and I am a primary school teacher working in Liverpool. Within my school I am part of the core faculty and I lead on Reading and Phonics.

I have always been passionate about books and almost exclusively read children's literature. I enjoyed reading from an early age and, although there were many books I could enjoy, there were very few books I could personally relate to. Being from an ethnic minority group, I rarely saw people who looked like me represented in books, the media, or anywhere else for that matter, and I really struggled with my identity because of it. I believe that all children deserve to see themselves reflected in society and this starts in the classroom.

There are now more books than ever with all kinds of inclusive representation. As teachers, we have a responsibility to use them as tools, not only so that children can see themselves in the stories we share, but also so that others can see them, too. So much can be done to overcome prejudice and bias by having simple conversations and there's no better catalyst for these discussions than a good book.

ABOUT ME: DOAA AL-SORAIMI

My name is Doaa Al-Soraimi and I am also a primary school teacher based in Liverpool.

My passion for books was sparked around the age of eight or nine, when English was a foreign language to me. The first book I read was *Matilda* and I found myself faced with my first page-turner. I used to read a chapter before bed each night and genuinely looked forward to going to sleep because of that half-hour of reading I would sneak in beforehand. As a child who was learning a new language, reading played a significant role in developing my knowledge of the language. I also used to read Arabic books, which meant that both languages were simultaneously improving.

Reading saved my identity as an Arab and allowed me to fit into a society that was foreign to me at the time. I'm passionate about representation in literature as I feel that it benefits reluctant readers more than anyone. When I suggest a book to a reluctant reader, I always suggest something that represents them in some way. This always resonates, leading to the child coming back to me for more recommendations. Having books (and a curriculum) that represents you can make or break your passion for learning.

ABOUT ME: ASHLEY BOOTH

I'm Ashley and I work alongside Jazz and Doaa within a trust of six schools in Liverpool. In my school, I lead on Teaching and Learning, and am also Reading Lead across the wider trust. During the past couple of years I have developed a whole-class reading curriculum, which includes a bank of over three hundred lessons. Having shared this online, I went on to run training throughout the summer of 2020 for teachers who were keen to try a similar approach in their schools.

As a child, I was diagnosed with ADHD. This is one factor (among many) that informs my passion for representation in all its forms, whether that is special needs, ethnicity, sexuality, poverty or mental health issues, among others. Children deserve to see themselves reflected in the curriculum they experience in school.

Having worked in a particularly deprived area of Liverpool (with a large majority of ethnic minority pupils), I have been able to see the positive impact of representation in children's literature first-hand. When children feel represented, they also develop a strong sense that they belong.

JASMINE NEWTON, DOAA AL-SORAIMI AND ASHLEY BOOTH: THE INTERVIEW

During the summer of 2020, worldwide events such as the Black Lives Matter movement triggered a lot of important conversations about representation in the curriculum. Many school leaders used this time as an opportunity to consider whether the school experiences we provided for our pupils went far enough in terms of representing a diversity of perspectives.

At this time, we came across Jasmine Newton, a Year 4 teacher based in Liverpool. Jazz had shared a brilliant resource on Twitter: an enormous PowerPoint file with hundreds of book suggestions that represented a diverse range of characters. Inspired by this, we set up a conversation with Jazz and her colleagues, Doaa and Ashley. The conversation focused on the idea of representation within children's literature, but the points made within it can be applied more holistically to our daily work in schools. While ethnicity was a pertinent aspect of this conversation, it is crucial to emphasise that representation is a broad issue that encompasses every unique perspective you can think of when it comes to being human.

> *I never saw myself represented in books as a child.*

As a child, Jazz never saw herself represented in books. As two white males in Western society, we have consistently seen ourselves represented in popular culture, in books, in advertisements, in positions of power and in thousands of other positive forms throughout our lives. As a result of being so well represented, we have been given the message that we matter, that we are valued, that we are deserving of success and that we are 'normal'. Conversely, what must it feel like if you don't see yourself represented throughout your life? It can make you feel as though you are unwanted, less important, less likely to succeed and less 'normal'. As Jazz said in her 'about me' section: this led to her experiencing a crisis of identity. When we first began to understand this perspective, it hammered home the message that *every* young person deserves to receive the message that they are important, that they are special and that they belong in our society. It is not good enough to dismiss this as an issue that only affects a few people, nor is it good enough to see it as a niche topic that we can consider as an afterthought. Representation is core to every child's experience of school life.

> *Representation is not only seeing myself, but seeing other people. When you don't know something, you are afraid of it because it's different. You tend to either run away from it or attack it.*

Doaa reminded us that representation goes beyond seeing oneself reflected in books and the wider curriculum. It is about having an open window through which to learn about experiences and perspectives that are distinctly different from our own. One of the many purposes of education surely has to be to nurture thoughtful, compassionate and curious young people who are open to learning about the experiences of others. Sadly, when children have a narrow educational experience, in which representation hasn't been considered, their reservoir of compassion and understanding may be limited in capacity. Unfortunately, these issues will only be exacerbated further for children who have a particularly blinkered upbringing.

Doaa explained that people have a fight or flight reaction to things that are different or unusual to them. She said in the podcast that the flight response (of ignoring an individual who is different from them) can be just as harmful or distressing as the more aggressive and abusive reaction. No child that we teach should ever feel that they have to hide away from their true identity.

> *Where do our children see themselves in a book where a character doesn't have any money and at the end they don't get given a chocolate factory? Life isn't going to give our children a chocolate factory and so they need to see themselves just existing.*

Ashley was speaking about young people who come from poorer economic backgrounds. He was making the point that representation can't be singular in its nature, nor should it always be about portraying a 'magical' ending. While we're sure that most educators would agree that *Charlie and the Chocolate Factory* is a wonderful story, children from backgrounds such as Charlie Bucket need to see themselves represented in a very 'normal' sense – just existing.

There is a slight danger that individuals who in some way belong to a minority group are only ever portrayed as victims of their circumstances. Stories of hope can be incredibly uplifting and they can give children a strong sense of agency. But if children only see stories written in this vein, they can inadvertently be given the message that there is something wrong with them and that they need saving from their circumstances. In the podcast, Ashley made the point that representation in the curriculum is as much about valuing people's normal lived experiences as it is about wonderful stories of hope or adventure. Both perspectives play their part, but both are needed if we are going to make children feel truly appreciated.

> *We need to move away from the tokenistic 'Let's have an Africa week!'*

As we wrestle with this issue of representation, there is a natural temptation to do things that seemingly tick the 'diversity box', and schools are prone to fall into this trap because we are so obsessed with compliance and being seen to be doing the right thing. Out of this sense of duty, we might suggest things like 'Let's have an Africa week!' or 'Maybe we should add a diversity section to the library?' or 'Let's put a few more ethnic minority figures into the curriculum'. All these activities are well-meaning, but they can be symptomatic of teachers and leaders missing the point somewhat.

An acid test of our diversity initiatives might be to consider how they would look if they were applied to a group in society that is in no way marginalised or rarely made to feel different. For example, would we ever think to have a 'books about white people' section of the library? It might seem like a crude comparison, but this is how tokenistic gestures can leave underrepresented people feeling. True representation is about fully embracing a diversity of perspectives and threading this through *all* that we do: our curricula, our word choices, our teaching resources, our conversations, our classroom environments, and so on. In schools where representation is a real strength, it is seen as a central thread of their work rather than a tick-box exercise. It is so embedded and natural that it's almost difficult to notice.

> *The worst possible thing you can do is just shy away from it and not do it all. The easiest thing you can do is ask someone who will know.*

When Jazz said these words, it really resonated for us both. As white men, we both related to that insecure, niggly feeling of 'I don't want to say the wrong thing or offend anyone'.

Yet the very existence of this podcast episode was evidence of the connectedness we have available to us in education and the numerous channels through which we can become more informed about issues such as representation. Our guests in this episode offered us three perspectives that were distinctly different from our own. They gave us food for thought, books to read and answers to some of our burning questions. In this comment, Jazz was reminding us that we are living in a world where answers are easily available to us if we are willing to look for them. We may work in a school that is not very diverse or where there isn't an expert on a given issue. This is no excuse for burying our heads in the sand on the issue of representation. You only have to pop on to the educational realms of social media sites and there will be someone who can answer your questions or who can point you in the right direction of a fantastic resource that might help you.

> *If I had read it when I was younger, it would have changed my life.*

Towards the end of the interview, each guest offered us some book suggestions that meant a lot to them, and we suggest that you listen to the podcast after reading this chapter as there are some brilliant titles mentioned. In the quotation above, Doaa was thinking about the book by author and Olympic athlete Ibtihaj Muhammad called *Proud: Living My American Dream*. We should say at this point that Ibtihaj also wrote the wonderful book *The Proudest Blue: A Story of Hijab and Family*, which we are glad to see is becoming a more common text in school libraries up and down the country. When discussing the book *Proud*, Doaa explained how important it was for her to read about a Muslim woman who wears a hijab, and all the incredible challenges and difficulties she had been through on her road to Olympic success. Doaa was inspired to read the story of someone who seemed similar to her, going on to be so successful in a sporting world where Muslim women are often so underrepresented. In the interview, Doaa suggested that if she had been able to read about Ibtihaj's story as a child, it would have completely shifted her beliefs about what she could do with her own life. Doaa told us that she would have had greater aspirations, instead of waiting to reach adulthood before developing the confidence to pursue her own dreams.

For us, Doaa's reflection about *Proud* is such a powerful illustration of the power of representation. Feeling represented is about feeling recognised, valued and empowered. Surely that is something every child deserves to feel during their time in school?

RUSSELL'S REFLECTION

If you want to focus more on the issue of representation, a helpful starting point is to admit that you have a blinkered view of the world, informed by your own life experiences. As a result of your upbringing, background and education, you will have unconscious biases that inform what you notice, what you are drawn to and what you value. I think it is our duty to acknowledge this as fact, and then to commit to challenging our own misconceptions and stereotypes so that the children we teach grow up to see the world through a more informed lens than perhaps we did.

As I have reflected on this topic of representation, I've kept my eyes peeled for indicators about how we're doing in my school when it comes to this issue. Negative indicators might include things such as children displaying negative stereotypes about another religion, culture or ethnicity. While I understand that such views sometimes stem from outside school, it is important to me that our curriculum provides ample opportunities for teachers to foster a respect in our pupils for people who are in some way different from them. When I hear examples of prejudice in my school, I like to look further upstream and ask: 'When did this prejudice first develop?'; 'What opportunities have we missed to tackle this viewpoint?'

Aside from negative indicators, there are, of course, the positive signs that we are doing a good job on the issue of representation. For me, a strong indicator that we're doing well is when children feel comfortable to talk about their unique identities with their peers and teachers. As part of this reflection, I would like to share two examples where I have seen this happen, and the beautiful role that individual teachers have played in these scenarios.

Imagine a class where a child follows a particular religion. Due to their faith, her parents have requested that they do not participate in RE lessons. Every time they leave the classroom before these lessons, other children become more curious about why that person doesn't stay in for RE. They want to know more about the religion that this child follows. One day, the pupil in hand approaches the teacher and says, 'Miss, people always ask me why I leave the class during RE. Do you think I could do a little presentation to the class about my religion and I can answer some of their questions?' Now, there are two parts of this narrative that I find interesting. The first is that this child feels safe enough to ask their teacher this question. This tells me that the culture of the class is one where the teacher clearly values her pupils and where they feel that she will listen to what they have to say. The second thing I find touching about this story is that the pupil knows that the other children won't be critical or cruel about her faith, otherwise she wouldn't ask to stand up in front of them and share such personal information. The class climate means that children listen to and respect each other's perspectives. This hasn't been established because of a special 'day'; it is core to how the class operates. So the teacher happily agrees and they co-plan this little lesson. A few days later, the girl delivers her RE lesson to the class and the children absorb it all enthusiastically. The next day, I cover the class for PPA and I ask them to tell me what they can remember from their RE lesson the day before. I am bombarded with interesting facts about the religion, all of which the girl nods along to approvingly. For the whole time, she is sitting with the biggest smile on her face. She has been heard. She has been noticed. She has been valued.

Only a few months after this event, another positive indicator hits home and tells me that perhaps we're getting the culture right in terms of representation. A wonderful pupil – a refugee who had escaped the war in Syria a few years ago – approaches her teacher to tell her that she is going to be doing a speech about her experiences somewhere locally at the weekend. This pupil hasn't been with us for long, but she feels safe to share this event with her teacher and the class as a whole. Now, before I continue with this anecdote, I want to talk about what I'd observed of this pupil–teacher relationship in the months ahead of this conversation. Since the pupil joined our school, she has been made to feel loved and wanted. Her teacher has been unfalteringly warm and has embraced her culture, background and religion at every opportunity. During Eid, this teacher provides constant words of encouragement and understanding (the pupil is trying to fast for the first time). At the end of this period, when the fast is broken, the pupil brings to school individually wrapped sweet treats for all her peers, because she knows this will be fine and that the teacher will support her in sharing the importance of this event with the class. Now, let's return to the speech story. The teacher praises her bravery for doing such a thing and shares the details about the speech in the assembly that week. Because of this, other classes end up discussing what it means to be a refugee and children break into impromptu applause because they admire their fellow student's courage. That weekend, the pupil's teacher and teaching assistant both go along, on a Saturday, to watch her give that speech.

When I saw the video of that girl speaking, I blubbed, not only because of the inspiring story she told, but because of the pride with which she spoke and the knowledge that her teachers were standing in front of her during the whole experience. Representation is beyond the books we choose, the curricula we design or the special days we have. It is tied up in the incredible relationships we nurture in our schools.

STEVE'S REFLECTION

This wonderful conversation came at a hugely important point of 2020, when the spotlight was shining brightly on the issue of representation. In this podcast, we were able to reflect deeply on how we promote representation within the walls of our schools and it made me keen to look ahead to creating a better future for the young people in my care. I was left with some burning questions after the interview, though: 'Was representation tokenistic in my school?' 'Did we have a broad book collection reflecting our communities and those beyond?' 'Were my colleagues confident in tackling ignorance and prejudice?'

The school I have worked in since I was an NQT has always had community at its heart. Indeed, it is a beautiful community with a plethora of cultures and we have always been keen to celebrate this. Each year we hold an event called 'Multicultural Week', during which every year group learns about different cultures within our community. Parents and families attend school to share information about their cultures and backgrounds, and it all culminates in 'Food Friday', when the school building and playground are transformed into mouth-watering market stalls, celebrating delicious foods from around the globe. I always saw this event as hugely positive; a chance to celebrate the diverse make-up of our community and to get everyone involved. To say that the week is full of happiness, energy and interest is quite an understatement, and it is one of the highlights of the year for colleagues, children and parents.

After the podcast, it made me wonder if this event is tokenistic in nature. On reflection, I think that our celebratory week is genuinely a meaningful and special part of the broad picture of representation. However, if this was to be the limit of our work on representation, then it would simply not go far enough – children would forget what they had learnt after a matter of weeks. It would be easy for children's appreciation of different countries and cultures to fade. They may not continue to make meaningful links if we didn't provide other opportunities within the curriculum and it would be easy to see Multicultural Week as a way of compartmentalising diversity into one neat week of the year. I am proud to say that this event sits within a wider context of representation in my school.

While I can reflect positively on this event, it is equally important to reflect on how representation could be a stronger feature of my school. Representation needs to be threaded continually throughout the curriculum and the culture of the school. There is a danger in trying to rush this process and see it as a bolt-on, which is unhelpful and ends up being a tokenistic response. This episode made me think hard about the power of books in normalising a diverse range of perspectives. Reading is quite the superpower, so for children to have the ability to pick up a book where they can relate to the character is the first step forward in representation being natural within school. Exposing children to books that have them see into other worlds is equally as important, and these texts shouldn't be seen as an odd or unusual choice for our children to make. I once shuddered when I heard of a school that had its own diversity corner in the library. I was pleased to see they had diversified their texts, but the fact that they were put in a stand-alone corner of the library was a concern. Books with diverse characters belong alongside every other book we want the children to read.

However well we do on representation, we will all be faced with situations when children say something that reflects a form of prejudice or ignorance about others. Getting the culture of representation right involves staff feeling comfortable to tackle such issues. My advice if this happens is to face it head-on, tackle the issue directly and make sure you educate children when they display ignorance on a particular issue. While some children may be trying to cause intentional harm, more often their comments reflect a lack of understanding, and it is our duty to help them to know better and do better. These issues don't only arise in areas where there is a lack of diversity, but, as our guests said in the episode, issues can be just as severe where there are frictions within a diverse community. Tackling examples of discrimination doesn't have to be done alone – in fact, the easiest thing to do would be to talk to someone who can support you with this. This could be from within school or from the wider education community. I always feel fortunate to be able to connect with educators online, and gain support and advice when there is a lack of expertise in the school itself.

Sometimes children observe a difference in others and feel the urge to comment on it. This is where books can play such a special part in promoting respect and understanding. They provide a safe space to discuss issues of race, heritage, discrimination and inequality, whether it is in an English, History or PSHE lesson, or just as a 'read for pleasure' book at the end of the day. Use this precious time to speak about difference and diversity, but also as a space within which diverse characters can just exist, completely normally.

YOUR REFLECTION

Take some time to digest what you've read during this chapter. We have provided some question prompts that you may like to consider, depending on your current role or level of experience.

Support staff

- You are an important role model to children when it comes to representation. Do you proudly share information about your own heritage, culture and background? This will inspire children to feel they can share, too.
- You play a vital role in illuminating information about pupils' backgrounds that they may feel nervous to share in school. How can you encourage children to feel confident to share special information about their own heritage? Do you actively show an interest in their hobbies, religious festivals or cultural activities outside school?
- It is likely in your role that you will see examples of discrimination – perhaps when on duty on the playground. It is vital that you take this seriously and feel that you can challenge this head-on. What is the best thing you feel that can do if you hear a child making a discriminatory remark to a peer?

Trainee teachers

- During your placements, it is likely that you will see schools with very different make-ups. Some may be more diverse than others, or they may reflect very different economic pictures in particular communities. How do the teachers and leaders embrace their school communities and give children a sense that they are important, regardless of background? What can you learn from this?
- Now is a great opportunity to broaden your experience of children's literature. Could you use online platforms to reach out to other teachers and ask for recommendations of diverse books to read?
- In terms of your future classroom environment, how could you represent a diverse range of role models from society? For example, does your Science display include some famous scientists from different ethnicities/religions/genders? This can be a simple way to challenge stereotypes such as 'scientists are always white men'.

Teachers

- Have a look at your book corner. How well does the range of books reflect both the diversity within your classroom and also in wider society? If it doesn't, can you seek support from your SLT to refresh the book corner so that it does a better job in this regard?
- In your classroom, do you regularly use opportunities to celebrate role models from a diverse range of backgrounds? Do you go out of your way to acknowledge those who have been successful in fields where they haven't fitted into a stereotypical mould?
- In your classroom, what space do you carve out within lessons such as RE and PSHE to celebrate the pupils' different perspectives? How can you foster a deep respect among your children for those with a different viewpoint from theirs?

Senior leaders

- With this focus on representation, are there any subjects within your curriculum that need a fresh look? For example, does your history curriculum portray a wide range of historical perspectives? Does your PSHE curriculum explicitly explore diversity in all its forms?
- Is any training needed with staff about the importance of representation within school life? Do you feel that staff have a thorough understanding of the community they serve and the diversity within it?
- Within the assembly programme, are you using this as an opportunity to celebrate (and show respect for) a diversity of perspectives? Stories are a powerful tool here. Remember the importance of sharing examples of diverse characters simply existing, rather than always overcoming adversity or escaping a particular circumstance.

CHAPTER 6

GENDER EQUALITY

LINKED PODCAST EPISODES:
Gender Equality (Parts 1 and 2)

GUESTS:
Graham Andre and Nic Ponsford

IN THIS CHAPTER WE EXPLORE:

- issues around gendered terms of endearment;
- being aware of unconscious biases related to gender;
- the importance of equal opportunities in the school environment.

ABOUT ME: GRAHAM ANDRE

I am a primary school teacher and Assistant Head working on the Isle of Wight. I have always worked in the education sector, starting as a Teaching Assistant and having various roles before doing a part-time degree and completing my GTP ten years ago.

I am a keen Twitter user, which helped to start and grow the #PrimaryRocks group, and has now held four sold-out teaching events. In 2017, I was seen working with my Year 3 class on the BBC2 documentary *No More Boys and Girls: Can Our Kids Go Gender Free?* Through this documentary, I have been invited to speak on national television, live events and various podcasts to discuss its impact. I am also a founding member of the Global Equality Collective which is doing great work in promoting equality in schools, homes and businesses.

ABOUT ME: NIC PONSFORD

I am now an educational and technology thought leader, having previously been an Advanced Specialist teacher, an award-winning teacher and Harvard author (*TechnoTeaching: Taking Practice to the Next Level in a Digital World*).

While studying for my doctorate, I have recently been an EdTech50 judge, head hunted for a central role with the DfE EdTech Demonstrator Programme, a white paper research analyst for HE and a freelance Online Learning Designer. I am Director of EdTech UK, the national independent organisation, advisory forum and strategic body, and I am also Editor of the digital publication, *Edtech UK Magazine*.

I am a frequent keynote speaker and panellist on closing gaps for the most vulnerable, #techforgood & #futureofwork, and all things regarding diversity and inclusion in education. I believe that technology is the great equaliser for our time.

GRAHAM ANDRE AND NIC PONSFORD: THE INTERVIEWS

In 2017, we vividly remember watching the BBC2 documentary *No More Boys and Girls: Can Our Kids Go Gender Free?* The documentary allowed the viewer to witness the steep learning curve of a very normal and lovely classroom teacher – Graham Andre – as he wrestled with issues of gender equality in his primary classroom. Facilitating the series was Dr Javid Abdelmoneim, who was keen to explore whether the way we treat boys and girls is the real reason we haven't yet achieved equality between men and women. The way in which he did this was to take over Graham's class, challenging many of his daily practices and carrying out a series of experiments. It remains a brilliant and accessible watch, and we really suggest you devour this short series after enjoying this chapter of the book. Almost four years after the documentary, we recorded an episode with Graham to allow him to reflect back on the experience and to consider how much things had (or hadn't) changed since.

In the episode with Graham, he referred to an organisation called the Global Equality Collective, which is headed up by Cat Wildman and Nic Ponsford. Cat and Nic came together not long after the BBC2 documentary with an ambitious vision of supporting schools and businesses to tackle issues of inequality, including those related to gender. Nic had a background in education, so we were keen to hear her voice on this matter too. In August 2021, we recorded Part 2 of this episode, which further enhanced our thinking on this matter.

Issues of inequality affect *everybody*. As educators, we have a moral responsibility to ensure that every child has the very best opportunities to do well in their education and to be the people that they want to be. We have not yet achieved gender equality in schools. It is such a vast issue, and like every other chapter in this book, this is simply an introduction to some key points that arose during our interviews with our guests. We hope that it fires you up to want to learn more – and to do more – when it comes to this important issue.

> The first thing that had to change was my use of terms of endearment in the classroom, because every time I said to a boy, 'mate' or 'fella', or to a girl, 'love' or 'sweet pea', it meant that I was saying that they were different.

Like many teachers, Graham had an ingrained habit when it came to terms of endearment, and it was clear that these terms were applied based on the gender of the children in his class. While Graham was aware of this, watching the documentary back shocked him as he hadn't realised quite how much he was doing it. When we discussed this with him, it was clear that these terms were used because Graham wanted to build positive relationships with his pupils and he was concerned that stopping this habit would affect those relationships negatively. Graham told us that the turning point in the documentary was hearing the children discussing this issue. It became apparent that the terms being used caused the boys and girls to think very differently about themselves and each other. After this hit home, Graham worked hard to stop using terms of endearment, and now says that he hasn't noticed any negative impact in doing so.

After discussing this with teachers we knew, it was interesting to see how perceptions differed between ourselves and some of our female colleagues. For example, it seemed (in our experience) that as men in the primary setting, we tended to use more gendered terms of endearment, whereas our female colleagues tended to use certain terms more universally for both boys and girls. We wondered whether (unconsciously) men in the primary setting felt as though they needed to soften themselves to the girls to appear more nurturing and use terms like 'buddy' or 'mate' with the boys as a way to build trust. This is, of course, madness, but nevertheless probably what was happening in our classrooms. In contrast, some of our female colleagues (like Russell's in Devon) talked about using quite regional terms such as 'lovely' for both boys and girls. When we interviewed Nic a few months later, we were keen to hear her take on this issue. Nic reflected on her own experience and said that in the secondary setting, she also used a lot of gendered terms as a way to try to build trust and rapport with her pupils. She also said that she remembered using other terms more universally, such as 'poppet'. Nic went on to point out that there is value in asking young people about their viewpoints on such matters. Do the children themselves feel comfortable being referred to as 'lovely' or 'poppet'? Are there certain terms everyone is happy with in our schools or are we best sticking to names? It's food for thought.

Regardless of your opinions on this matter, it's healthy to stop and consider whether the terms you use with children are likely to reinforce gender stereotypes. Subtle changes in our language can have a huge impact over time. It is important to realise that the way we interact with children is likely to be based, in part, on our own unconscious biases and stereotypes. This means that we may treat boys and girls differently without even realising it, purely because of our own upbringing and the influences in our lives.

> I started my own science experiment. I have five-year-old twins. My son is very kind and caring and he carries his soft toys around, whereas my daughter will do a warrior cry and run at the trampoline at full force!

In this quotation, Nic was reflecting on her experience of raising boy–girl twins and how it has been interesting to see the natural characteristics they have each developed in early childhood. She also talked about how teachers and other adults have such a profound influence on children's tastes and interests – often based on the adults' perceptions of what they *think* girls or boys will like.

In the documentary, there was a great little experiment where some babies/toddlers were dressed up in stereotypically boy/girl clothing (opposite to their actual sex). The producers then brought in some adults (who didn't know them) to play with them using a selection of toys that were laid out on a large carpet. What the experiment consistently showed was that the adults frequently pushed certain toys towards the children based on what they *thought* the children would like. The perception of a child's gender had a profound impact on how the adults treated these children, and this could be considered a microcosm of a wider societal issue. What is important to state is how shocked these adults were when the nature of the experiment was revealed to them. None of them were consciously pushing an agenda on to these young people. It was a great example of unconscious bias in action.

In terms of the school environment, this sort of thing can often show itself in the little things we say or do. As Graham said in the podcast, it can be simple things like a teacher saying after assembly, 'Are there any strong boys who can help me put the benches away?' Imagine the impact when boys and girls hear these messages from teachers and family members all throughout their childhood. What might the cumulative effect of this be when it comes to their interests and perceptions of themselves?

> *The thing that really shocked me was the way the girls perceived themselves in relationship to the boys, and how little they thought they could achieve, and be, and do.*

In Graham's Year 3 classroom, perceptions of what boys or girls could do were well established. Graham was particularly upset by how negatively his female pupils felt about what they could do and achieve. In the documentary, Graham observed that many of the girls in his class had very low self-esteem and significantly underestimated what they could do, particularly when it came to physical activity. The boys, in contrast, often overestimated their potential and this was best illustrated in a 'strength competition' which took place out on the playground – the poignant highlight of the documentary, in our eyes.

After realising how little Graham's female pupils thought of themselves, he became determined to open their eyes to what they *could* do and achieve. This was in part an issue of opportunity.

> *It is about giving children equal opportunities to do everything. So let girls use Lego and be creative and build things, and climb trees, and let boys be nurturing, and natural, and do ballet and dance. If they try these things and find they don't like them, then that's fine.*

One of the big shifts for Graham was wanting to create a school environment in which *all* children felt that they could try anything and be anything. When he now talks about his school, there is a much broader range of opportunities available for children and the engagement in clubs is balanced when it comes to gender. For Graham and his colleagues, they have realised that one of the practical things they can do is to be proactive in putting on a wide range of opportunities for their students. As Graham says, 'If they turn out not to like something – fine! But at least we've given them that chance to try.'

When we spoke to Nic about the topic of opportunity, she emphasised the danger of leaving this work until children are much older. She was reflecting on initiatives aimed at teenagers or young adults and said, 'It gets too late when you are getting to that stage. This is about Early Years and primary school, when we start to enforce those messages that you can be what you want.' This is a great example of how profoundly important the work of Early Years colleagues is. From the moment we have young people in our care, we can either work to reinforce or challenge harmful stereotypes around gender. There are so many wonderful Early Years settings up and down the country helping our youngest pupils to see that they can do and be anything that they like. It's so important we get this right from the word go and then sustain it throughout a child's education.

> *I like to go beyond the 'see it to be it'. I want kids to be pioneers; they can be the first.*

In Part 2 of the podcast, we were discussing the part that role models play in helping children to see that they can do or be anything. This can really help when it comes to shifting perceptions about 'boy' or 'girl' subjects, which is still a real issue within education and many professions. We talked about the profound difference that female teachers can make in building positive perceptions in girls about sports or STEM (Science, Technology, Engineering and Mathematics) subjects, for example. Just by modelling a positive attitude about a particular subject, teachers can shift pupils' attitudes quite significantly. Equally, as male teachers in the primary setting, we have seen time and time again how important it is for both the boys and girls to see us acting kindly, compassionately and gently – characteristics that some children might not consider important, or normal, for men to exhibit.

We went on to discuss the idea that 'you can't be what you can't see' – a term often used when people discuss about the power of representation. However, Nic's response above was just magic. In her work, she is inspired to help children to see that sometimes they might just be the first; to be that pioneer who 'breaks through' a particular barrier. What if schools can help young people to deeply believe this too?

RUSSELL'S REFLECTION

Every form of inequality in our schools needs careful consideration, and Nic's organisation, the GEC, is a great starting point for any school wanting to do better when it comes to equality, diversity and representation. To have the opportunity to focus specifically on issues related to gender was so interesting for Steve and me, and in my reflection I want to consider how those little things we do and say to children can make a massive difference to what they think they can be and do.

I am now in the privileged position of co-leading on curriculum design in my school. This is an often terrifying and overwhelming feat, but it is also such a privilege to design the educational journey that our pupils will experience. When we came to reviewing our curriculum a few years ago, we knew that there were some units that we definitely wanted to keep. For example, in Year 2, children had always learnt about Amelia Earhart in History.

Not only was this an interesting History unit, but we observed that our female pupils in particular became really fired up as a result of learning about her. One significant example of this occurred when I was sitting in the hall one day having lunch with a Year 2 pupil. This child had found the unit so exciting and it had piqued her interest when it came to engineering. 'Mr Pearson,' she said out of nowhere, 'I want to be the first girl to build a robot.' 'Oh,' I said (not knowing much about female robot engineers), 'what a great idea. Well, why don't you have a go at designing one?' She gave me a long, hard stare and then looked down at the table sadly. 'I just don't have any craft stuff to make one with.' At that point, I leapt up and we headed off to examine our Art/DT supplies. Within ten minutes we'd filled a whole bag (don't tell the School Business Manager) and I told her that I wanted her to have a go at designing that robot. Every time I saw this student for the next few months, I asked her about her progress. Eventually, one day she brought me a photograph that showed her standing proudly beside a very impressive (and massive) robot. I really believe this pupil can be a pioneer one day, in whatever she decides to do. I have no idea if this little event will have played a part in her future aims or ambitions, but as educators we *have* to believe that when we invest time in young people like this, we might just be lighting a very precious flame.

As a parent of two daughters, I've thought about gender equality a lot. I'm determined that my children won't ever have their chances diminished because of their gender, and yet I know that they will face challenges growing up. One challenge they have already encountered is regarding attitudes to sport. My eldest child has never really been into football, but one summer a close friend asked her to accompany her to a one-off training event locally and she was pleased to go along. However, when they arrived, they were the only two girls there in an enormous crowd of boys. My daughter was a little nervous, but went in with a smile and a positive attitude. Unfortunately, when I returned later to collect her, she told me that various boys had made negative remarks about them during the day and that they felt excluded throughout the training sessions. This was meant to be a really positive day, but sadly the events that occurred ended up reinforcing the idea that my child didn't belong there. It reminded me that children have a huge role to play in tackling (or reinforcing) gender inequality and that adults have to be on the ball in noticing these things happening. As educators, we have to be fiercely attuned to the language that children use about each other and firm in challenging any form of stereotyping being used in the classroom or on the playground. Our interventions in such matters can be the difference between children feeling deflated or inspired to try again. In the case of my incredible daughter, we talked things through and she bounced back quickly enough. She is a capable, confident young person who has a strong sense of agency about her future. But like every child, she deserves to be championed and encouraged throughout her childhood so that she doesn't put limits on what she can achieve in life.

Thinking back to the documentary, it had me really think about emotional literacy in children, but in boys in particular. In Graham's class, the girls had a significantly more developed vocabulary when it came to emotions, whereas the boys could only really talk about anger. This is my experience, too, and something I have worked hard to change as both a teacher and leader. There are various vehicles through which we can do this. First of all, there is the power of books, which are a great way of discussing difficult and complex issues in a way that is somewhat distanced for young people. A boy who finds it tricky to talk about emotions may find it easier to do so when discussing a character in a book. Try to thread emotional literacy through your 'book talk' as it really will benefit all children. This can, of course, happen through the PSHE curriculum, which I also think needs to be a huge driver for developing emotional literacy. As a male in the primary setting, I always let my pupils see an element of 'emotional vulnerability' in me when I teach a PSHE lesson. For example, when discussing body image with Year 6 pupils, I'll talk about sometimes feeling that my tummy is rather flabby and the pressure to look like the men on TV or social media. If I can't model emotional literacy, how can I expect the children to be open with me and each other?

STEVE'S REFLECTION

Having previously worked as a solicitor, I am really interested in supporting others to overcome the barriers in their lives, so gender inequality has been of particular interest. Having watched the documentary in 2017, it was fantastic to welcome Graham on to our podcast and then to be fortunate enough to also hear Nic's thoughts about this issue and the amazing work that the GEC does.

I found it particularly pertinent to discuss the terms of endearment used in the classroom and how this can have a negative impact on our children. I adore every class I teach and I love forming relationships with the children, finding out what their interests are and always thinking of my class as one big, happy family. In order to achieve this culture, I can reflect that I have previously used terms of endearment like 'mate' to boys in my class. I have also shortened first names or I have used nicknames like 'Ames' instead of 'Amy'. I guess my school was fairly laid back and informal, so using more colloquial terms around the children wouldn't have raised any eyebrows. However, over time I have changed in this respect. This is partly about moving into leadership, where I recognised that I would struggle to lead on behaviour while also calling children terms like 'mate', but it is also because I have learnt about the potential negative impact of terms of endearment within school. Did I ever consider how these terms made children feel? Did it suggest to students that some of them were my 'favourites'? Did it really make much of a difference to the rapport I was trying to build? It is hard to know for certain, but what I do know is that I never want to say anything that would impact students negatively or to speak in a way that could be considered unprofessional. On reflection, I can see that, like Graham, I was unconsciously applying terms of endearment based on the gender of children. I understand now that this would likely cause the boys and girls to think differently about themselves and each other. Having since tweaked the language I use around school, I can say with confidence that it has had no negative impact on my relationships.

Another part of the podcast that resonated with me was about the importance of providing the same opportunities for all children, regardless of their gender. I have taught classes with a high girl to boy ratio (and vice versa), but on one occasion I had a particular class that was fairly equal in terms of the proportion of boys and girls. They were tricky in terms of behaviour and had experienced a lot of disruption and change in the years before I taught them. Having recently watched the documentary at the time, I felt inspired to try something new with them. At the time, the school was using a Golden Time reward system. We had trialled all sorts during this reward time: forest schools, team games on the field and my next proposal was for us to try some sewing, which I thought would be calming, as well as helping to improve pupils' fine motor skills. This idea raised some very interesting comments from parents about whether their son should do it, because supposedly 'he really doesn't want to'. In fact, several parents at the time commented that they saw it as too 'girly' for their child, and naturally some of the children expressed this view too. The easy option would have been to agree and dismiss the idea. However, I am of the opinion that sometimes we are too obsessed with pandering to the idea of 'immediate engagement', meaning we can avoid opportunities that might not hook every child straight away. Having stood strong on this initiative, I can honestly say that every child went on to enjoy it, regardless of their gender. There was no stereotyping as to who could (or shouldn't) sew, and the children bonded because they were each doing their little bit for a class collage. It reminded me that just because we have unconscious views about whether something is more masculine or feminine, we should never let this influence the opportunities we provide for young people.

This leads me to my final reflection – a memory triggered by Nic's 'scientific experiment' with her own children. I can remember a time when my school had a successful football team dominated by boys (many of whom were in my class), but there was also a girl in my class who I went on to discover was very talented, too. She was much smaller than most children, and the unconscious perception of both me and the other students was that she would not be very interested in football – perhaps because of her size, her gender and her other interests that we knew about. The following event would prove why it is so important not to pre-judge anyone's skillset based on these absurd factors. When I used to ask for role models to demonstrate a skill in PE lessons, I knew I had lots of boys from our school football team that I could draw on for pretty much any activity. However, I was becoming more conscious that in doing this, I was overlooking the potential in others. I remember such a profound moment when I chose this particular girl to demonstrate a football drill in a lesson, and she did so perfectly. I can remember how gobsmacked the boys (and staff) were about her 'hidden' talent. At the time, it sent such a healthy message to all the children that anyone can do anything, regardless of their gender. As teachers, so many of our decisions can be an opportunity to break down these gender barriers and to give students a massive boost to their confidence. This pupil's talent was only 'hidden' because I hadn't yet given her the opportunity to show it.

YOUR REFLECTION

Take some time to digest what you've read during this chapter. We have provided some question prompts that you may like to consider, depending on your current role or level of experience.

Support staff

- Do you ever slip into using gendered terms of endearment? How might this affect how the children perceive each other and also their relationships with you?
- During your duty times on the playground, how can you ensure that all children feel confident to participate in any activity, regardless of their gender? Do you challenge children when they refuse to include another child because they are a 'boy' or 'girl'?
- One finding of Graham's documentary was that boys really struggled to express their emotions. Can you think of a particular child in your class who finds this difficult? How could you support them to develop more confidence with expressing their feelings?

Trainee teachers

- During your placements, what do you notice about boys and girls, and how confident they are in expressing their emotions? Do you feel this has improved since Graham's documentary or does this remain a significant issue in schools today?
- When observing different classroom teachers, what do you notice about how they select children for different tasks in lessons? How do their choices affect the confidence of boys and girls within different subjects?
- During your training, it would be all too easy to make a habit of terms of endearment. Have you noticed yourself using any particular terms in class? What difference does it make when you choose not to use them?

Teachers

- Do you think you ever fall into the trap of using an 'obvious choice' of child to model a particular skill or piece of understanding? Is this ever bias to a particular gender – e.g. more weighted to boys in PE or girls in English? Is this something you could try to mix up more in future?
- When selecting tasks or literature for the class, do you ever make choices based on your perception of what 'boys' or 'girls' will engage with? Is this something you could move away from in future – e.g. Steve's example of trying sewing despite the fact that parents weren't so sure?
- We know that developing emotional literacy is key for both boys and girls. What opportunities are there for you to model your own emotional literacy throughout the normal school day?

Senior leaders

- In your role, you may hear colleagues talking about the challenges of 'boy-heavy' or 'girl-heavy' classes. How can you challenge this kind of thinking and support your staff to understand that this needn't be an issue?
- When it comes to curriculum design, do you think there has been any unconscious bias at play when it comes to the choices your team has made? For example, are books selected based on the gender balances of a particular class or are any themes chosen to 'appeal to the boys'?
- In your curriculum, do children get to learn about many people who were pioneers in a particular field? Do they get to see lots of examples of people being successful in areas where people of their gender hadn't been before?

CHAPTER 7

DISADVANTAGE

LINKED PODCAST EPISODE:
Unpicking Disadvantage – Sonia Thompson

GUEST:
Sonia Thompson

> **IN THIS CHAPTER WE EXPLORE:**
>
> - the drawbacks and benefits of the label 'disadvantaged';
> - the importance of evidence-informed, Quality First Teaching in improving outcomes for disadvantaged pupils;
> - developing and maintaining a 'high expectations' culture;
> - the idea that every child brings their own cultural capital with them to school.

ABOUT ME: SONIA THOMPSON

My name is Sonia Thompson and I am the Headteacher and Director of St Matthew's CE Primary Research and Teaching School in Nechells, Birmingham. It is a privilege to work in one of the most disadvantaged areas in the country and I am passionate about our children not being seen as 'deficit'. In fact, I am determined that our children have every opportunity to flourish.

At St Matthew's, we started our 'knowledge-driven', subject-specific curriculum journey in 2014. Our aim was to underpin our curriculum with rigour and equity, and embed our school's vision and values. Equally as important, we wanted to celebrate our children's diversity, not as an 'add on', but as part of our curriculum principles. We have worked hard at placing culture, curriculum, community and reading for progress and pleasure at the heart of the school.

We applied to become a Research School in order to deepen and strengthen our own evidence-informed practices as well as to support other schools. Within this, I am clear that context and local knowledge is critical if schools are to embed any evidence-informed practices. As a leadership team, our aim continues to be to leverage the research (best bets), alongside our contextual data, in order to equip our practitioners and children to become their very best selves, both socially and academically.

SONIA THOMPSON: THE INTERVIEW

The vast majority of educators will encounter pupils during their careers who will be considered 'disadvantaged'. For clarity, in this chapter we are referring to pupils who meet the criteria for Pupil Premium (PP) funding – a government grant designed to support schools in improving progress and outcomes for children from disadvantaged backgrounds. This includes any child who is in receipt of Free School Meals (FSM), or those who have been in receipt of FSM during the previous six years. The grant also includes funding for children who are looked after, meaning that the local authority has either full or shared parental responsibility for them. The existence of this grant is the result of a long-lasting and stubborn achievement gap between 'PP' and 'non-PP' students.

Every teacher has a moral responsibility to provide disadvantaged pupils with the very best education possible. Leaders have a critical role in this in that they must decide how to use their PP funding in order to improve outcomes for disadvantaged pupils in their schools. Keen to develop our own understanding of this topic further, we spoke to Headteacher Sonia Thompson about her views regarding this very issue. For context, at Sonia's school, around 50 per cent of pupils are eligible for Free School Meals. We wanted to speak to Sonia as she has a great track record of improving outcomes for her students, and she has also written and spoken extensively about the topic of disadvantage.

As Deputies who have each led on Pupil Premium, we hoped that we would learn a lot from this conversation with an experienced and inspirational Headteacher. We certainly weren't disappointed.

> *I am not about labels, but unfortunately that's what it takes to get some recognition.*

As soon as we use a single word to describe a large proportion of society, it can naturally seem that we are labelling a whole group of individuals as 'the same'. In addition, there's no avoiding the fact that a term like 'disadvantaged' is not a particularly positive one. As we touched on in Chapter 5, it is neither healthy nor appropriate to view children from less financially privileged backgrounds as in need of our pity or of rescuing.

In the podcast, Sonia told us that she would have been considered a 'disadvantaged pupil' based on her own circumstances growing up, so we were keen to ask her about how she felt about such a label. In her response above, you can see that she reluctantly acknowledged the role that a label can take in getting recognition for some of the problems poverty *can* bring. In the podcast, Sonia gave the example of the housing issues that are common in the community she serves. When there are issues with a family's accommodation, there are natural knock-ons for the young people living there. In an area such Nechells, there can be very negative connotations about the community itself. This can leave some young people who live there feeling as though their life chances are more limited than those who are perhaps from a more financially privileged background. Some young people have to deal with very different circumstances from another child in their class who has never had to worry about issues like insecure housing, overcrowding or where their next meal is going to come from.

> *Disadvantage doesn't mean deficit. We're not dealing with children who haven't got brains and abilities and ambitions and dreams. It is how we can support children to move that forward.*

Sonia was very clear that disadvantaged children should not be viewed as empty vessels or as individuals who don't want to do anything important with their lives. Intelligence is not determined by our postcode or upbringing, so it is vital that educators do not see it this way. In addition, we must be so careful not to indulge lazy stereotypes about the type of care that children from financially poorer households receive. When Sonia described her own upbringing, it was quite clear that her parents had very high expectations for her education. Any teacher knows that the love, support and attention a child receives at home does not directly correlate to how poor or wealthy their family is.

Sonia was calling on us to see every child that we work with as an individual with hopes and dreams, and it is our mission to remove as many barriers for our students as possible. So what *can* schools do to support disadvantaged children to succeed educationally? What will make the greatest difference to them being able to achieve their goals?

> *Where we talk about disadvantaged pupils, we often talk about interventions and often that means children coming out of classrooms. I am not a great believer in interventions in that way. I am a believer in empowering the person who has those children the most, which is the class teacher. It always boils down to Quality First Teaching – that's what the research says.*

One thing that Sonia Thompson is known for is her belief that schools should be evidence-informed organisations. We will be saying a lot more about this in our final chapter, but Sonia was making the point that schools need to avoid wasting time on the things that will make little or no difference to pupil outcomes. In the example above, Sonia is tackling the common practice of children being sent out of class to do interventions. She was not saying that a specific, targeted intervention has no role in a child's education, but was critiquing the common practice of children being sent out of the class (with a less qualified colleague) for large chunks of the school day. As incredible as support staff can be, the teacher is the most qualified adult to deliver the teaching, and therefore the most important person that disadvantaged pupils need to work with. Disadvantaged pupils need regular access to the teacher's daily high-quality teaching.

In the podcast, Sonia made reference to the EEF (Education Endowment Foundation) which has published extensive guidance on how schools can develop an evidence-informed approach to their PP strategy. It is very clear in this guidance (and echoed on the government's own website) that the first 'tier' of any PP approach should be for schools to focus on improving the quality of teaching in the school. While we did not have time to examine every aspect of effective teaching, we did discuss two things that Sonia is particularly passionate about: reading and a culture of high expectations.

> *The evidence says that reading for progress and reading for pleasure go hand in hand.*

Sonia is extremely passionate about literacy and has extensive experience in research and training regarding the role of reading for pleasure (RfP) in a child's education. Sonia believes passionately that children who read for pleasure, and do so because of their own desire to read, are more likely to achieve well and make good progress academically.

In the podcast, Sonia acknowledged that there has been a problematic history of reading for pleasure being edged-out of the timetable due to other pressures. However, she acknowledged that this is gradually changing as more schools are seeing the power that reading for pleasure can have on pupils' attitudes and outcomes. For example, simply making the daily class story-time sacrosanct is one way of ensuring that every child in your classroom experiences high-quality literature on a daily basis. Not only will it improve pupils' attitudes to books, but they will be absorbing new vocabulary, improving their knowledge of the world and hearing what fluent reading sounds like. The value of this for all children – but particularly those from disadvantaged backgrounds – is huge.

Sonia made the important point in the podcast that in order to support this RfP culture teachers need to see themselves as readers. Not only that, but they also need to have a good understanding of children's literature in order to make recommendations to their students and engage in valuable 'book talk', too. This is something that doesn't come naturally to all teachers, so it is imperative that school leaders carve out time for teachers to engage with children's literature and the research about why it is so important. Equally, teachers need to understand that *their* attitudes to reading also play an enormous part in moulding their students' attitudes.

> All children must leave St Matthew's knowing that we've done our very best on our leg of the journey, and when we hand the baton over to the secondary schools, we can be confident that we've done what we need to do.

One thing that is clear about Sonia is the high expectations she holds for herself, her staff and her children. We were keen to know why this is so important and how she has worked to establish this in her school.

Sonia's team clearly has a very deep caring for the pupils in their care. One could argue that this is the case in all schools, but perhaps in some school communities this is 'lived and breathed' in a way that is more intentional. In Sonia's school, one way this shows itself is in the good behaviour that her pupils display. All staff have high expectations for behaviour, and clear systems are so well embedded that this does not pose an obstacle to pupils' achievement. Behaviour is a very important issue when it comes to disadvantaged pupils' progress. They deserve to work in an environment where they are able to concentrate without frequent interruptions due to poor behaviour. As well as this, Sonia talked about how much her school had pared back on the things that make little difference to pupils' outcomes. So while she and her staff may work very hard, it's not about working ridiculous hours or doing things just for the sake of it. Instead, it's about putting their energies into the things that make the most difference to a child's education. Once again, this is where the role of research has made a big difference to the working practices in Sonia's school. Energies are focused on the 'best bets' about what approaches are most likely to make the difference to pupils' outcomes.

Everybody has something in terms of a culture, regardless of how small or how big they feel it is. And it is within that culture that you will find some really important things to that family that have made them who they are. I would call that cultural capital.

A final aspect of the conversation that we found fascinating was Sonia's reflections on the phrase 'cultural capital'. This term causes much debate within the world of education. To some, it represents the assets of a person that enable them to achieve social mobility. To Sonia, cultural capital is not just about the knowledge that children inherit from school, but also about the unique culture and identity that every child brings with them when they walk through her school gates. She refers to this idea as the 'invisible backpack' – that is, the stuff that every child brings with them to school, but that they aren't always allowed to share once they get there. In the podcast, Sonia referred to her own childhood with regard to this issue. She talked about her home life and the focus on her Christian faith, learning about the Bible and the focus on oracy, reading and writing. She said that once she arrived at school, these aspects of her identity weren't 'seen' by her teachers, but rather she was just perceived as 'that girl from the big family'. In the podcast, Sonia talked about how they work hard at St Matthew's to amplify the lived experiences of the school community.

Here is a passage of text from the curriculum section Sonia's school's website:

At St Matthew's C.E. Primary School, we acknowledge and celebrate our children's heritage. Through becoming more open about our own experiences and literacy practices, we hope to build more reciprocal relationships and find out more about our children's individual passions, preferences, interests and practices both within and beyond school.

Coming full circle, we can see from this that Sonia does not have a deficit view of her school community. She and her staff believe that through a relational approach, where every family's experiences are valued, they can work together to support their students to excel.

RUSSELL'S REFLECTION

Like Sonia, I hate putting limits on what young people can achieve, and I enjoy the challenge of proving that *all* children can make great progress with the right support and high expectations. In my reflection, I will be considering two aspects that shone through in the interview with Sonia: the relationships we establish with families in our school community and the importance of supporting pupils' enjoyment of reading.

In my first school, I remember having little direct contact with pupils' parents. This was a daft geographical problem in that I taught in Year 6 and at the end of each day pupils would exit my class and dash up a short pathway to meet their parents, who had to wait about 15 feet from my classroom. As a result, I didn't engage in many daily chats with parents and therefore didn't realise the potential impact that regular communication could have on their progress. Then, when I moved to Steve's school, this all changed. I was to teach Year 4 and parents dropped off and collected from my (playground) classroom door. Immediately I noticed a huge difference: I was able to engage in regular conversations with parents, keeping them in the loop about their children's learning. I very quickly saw the trust that you establish when you make this effort. In this particular class, I taught a child (who would be considered disadvantaged) who had a long history of struggling with his behaviour in school. His mum was clearly used to hearing negative news from staff, so I made it my mission to break this cycle. From his very first day with me, I went out of my way to notice his successes and told his mum all about them at the end of each day. Her whole demeanour seemed to shift over a matter of days – she became excited to talk to me rather than dreading the encounter. And because of my efforts to praise her son, she took it well when I had to deliver some 'less positive' news. This was my first experience of seeing the power of a reciprocally caring relationship with a pupil (and their family) and the positive impact it can make on the child's progress in school. He did so well.

A few years later, after I moved to Devon as an Assistant Headteacher, I was put in charge of managing the Year 6 transition to secondary school. One pupil in particular had experienced a rather rocky Year 6 and unfortunately regularly found herself in trouble. I worked really hard to support her, both in terms of establishing a positive rapport, but just as importantly, by being really clear about my expectations. This was a real learning curve for me, because I was probably guilty in the past of allowing a disadvantaged pupil's out-of-school challenges to become the reason for them to underachieve. I absolutely needed to understand her home challenges and how those factors affected her behaviour in school, but I also needed to go out of my way to teach her very explicitly about what she needed to do in order to be successful as a learner and as a member of our school community. When it was almost time for this pupil to move up to Year 7, I discovered that her mother had been permanently excluded from the same secondary school that she was about to go to. Because of this, they were both naturally anxious about the same thing happening again, so I arranged a transition visit with us all going together to meet the Year 7 lead. As we walked around the high school, it was such a privilege to be that safe, trusted person who could help them to see that things were going to be OK. We need to remember that parents' experiences of school can have a massive impact on the feelings their children bring in to school with them, too. I have so many anecdotes like this, where investing time in understanding a family has paid dividends in terms of the future successes of the young person.

Finally, I want to reflect on the points that Sonia made about reading and teachers being role models in this respect. In the podcast I shared that my greatest regret as a teacher was not knowing enough about children's literature. I talked about a Year 6 teacher I have worked with more recently who devours children's books and who has established an incredible reading culture in her classroom. There are some very simple things I have observed her do that I thought I would share. First of all, she loves reading. She knows a lot about children's literature, meaning she is able to make bespoke recommendations for her pupils. When she talks about books, her eyes light up and, unsurprisingly, so do the children's. Her book corner is not flashy, but it is well organised and neat, and books are routinely rotated. When she spots a child picking a new book, she always engages in some book talk with them. 'Oooh,' I hear her say, 'good choice. I think I read this one as a child. Yes! What a great plot – good choice.' These little comments are so encouraging and imme-diately make the pupil's reading a more relational experience. She also actively monitors how they're doing with their new books, often popping over to certain individuals during silent reading time. 'Can I set you a little challenge?' I'll hear her say. 'Let's see if you can get to here today' and she will place a little post-it note on the target page. During the year I have seen children raise their hands and ask for these targets – what a simple idea, but so motivating for her pupils. I am sure she does so much more than what I have described here, but I wanted to reiterate Sonia's points about the correlation between reading for pleasure and reading for progress. In this colleague's classroom, children make superb pro-gress in reading because of the reading culture this teacher has established. These are simple approaches that have an enormous impact, particularly for her disadvantaged pupils.

STEVE'S REFLECTION

It was great to reflect on how best we can support children from disadvantaged back-grounds. Having previously been fortunate enough to lead on Pupil Premium at my school, I was looking forward to talking with Sonia about the teaching practices that could support my own school and to consider any tweaks we could make to improve outcomes for disad-vantaged pupils. In my view, the best 'take-away' from this episode was the simple and profound phrase: disadvantage doesn't mean deficit.

I have always had a passion for getting to know all my students as individuals and to ensure that they know there needn't be any boundaries to the progress they want to make. It didn't matter what their culture, heritage or background was, when they were at school they were seen as bringing great value. Just because a child was identified as 'pupil premium', this never meant to me that they would necessarily have lower ambitions or expectations. I remember overhearing discussions on a course I attended where someone said, 'It's like strik-ing gold when you teach a high-achieving pupil premium child.' I mean, that is *all kinds* of wrong. I repeat Sonia's words once more: disadvantage doesn't mean deficit. Whatever we do, let's never lower our expectations of any pupil because of their background. Children from disadvantaged backgrounds are more than capable of achieving great things, but it is Quality First Teaching that will get them there.

As Sonia rightly said, we should not be about labels, but unfortunately in order to get recognition and funding we are in a situation where they are necessary. However, the labels don't need to go beyond what they are required for. Children from disadvantaged back-grounds are not the empty vessels some perceive; they add value, culture and depth to the wonderful communities we work in. We are the lucky adults who can amplify their voices and their lived experiences, and we are in the privileged position of determining the quality of education they will receive. I loved Sonia's message about knowing when children leave our school that we have done our very best. As a school leader, I have been heavily involved in pupils' transition to secondary school. It really is a privilege to feel that we have provided the best opportunities for our children and to know that we've done what we needed to do in order to help them to succeed in their next steps.

A big consideration for me as a school leader has been what to do with additional funding or how best to support disadvantaged pupils. If we have the highest expectations for every child, can we really justify children being removed from the classroom to participate in intervention after intervention? I can reflect on the fact that this is something we have tried and tested at my school. In this model, the disadvantaged pupils and low prior attainers were regularly taken out by teaching assistants and worked in the corridor to try to accelerate their progress. The impact was simply non-existent. While targeted interventions do have a time and a place, we really need to appreciate the value of Quality First Teaching. If we invest funding in evidence-informed professional development, then that enhances teaching, leading to improvements in the classroom that will shift outcomes for all our children. So to anyone wanting to raise outcomes for disadvantaged pupils, focus on your daily teaching practices and systems. When we made this shift at my school, we saw an upturn in progress and attainment for all children. As well as this, pupil voice told us that children were happier in class with their teachers (and peers) and not missing areas of the curriculum they enjoyed most. The issues with interventions outside the classroom hit home when I noticed a pupil's absences increasing as they were asked to do phonics and reading interventions during PE twice a week. We failed to appreciate their talent and love for sports, and instead swapped this precious time for a little more phonics, something that had limited impact but negatively affected their attitude to school. It is so important to know your children well and to be mindful of the things that may motivate (or demotivate) them.

Finally, when thinking about unpicking disadvantage, remember that we are the role models at school. Having the highest expectations, showing compassion towards every child and really caring deeply must be the aim of every staff member. When our school communities feel that we are putting their needs first and valuing what they bring to the table, then we really do lay the solid foundations for improving outcomes for children from disadvantaged backgrounds.

YOUR REFLECTION

Take some time to digest what you've read during this chapter. We have provided some question prompts that you may like to consider, depending on your current role or level of experience.

Support staff

- Sonia talked about the importance of avoiding lots of 'out of the class' interventions. Is this something you are used to being asked to do? Could you discuss the idea of supporting a wider range of children back in class with your teacher?

- You may find that you are asked to work with disadvantaged pupils who, due to always being given a TA to work with, have developed some 'learnt helplessness'. How can you model high expectations of these children so that they learn to be more independent and confident in their own abilities?
- Excellent behaviour is key for disadvantaged pupils. How can you support the teacher in class to ensure a working environment that is calm and disruption-free?

Trainee teachers

- During your placements, what do you notice about the expectations that disadvantaged children have of themselves and their work? How does this affect what they produce in lessons?
- What do you notice about the impact of staff's expectations on these children's work? Do some teachers accept more or less than others? How might this impact the most disadvantaged pupils?
- Try to keep your expectations high at all times. Part of this is to ensure that children's behaviour is of a high standard in your lessons. Do you always state your expectations before children begin a task? Do you always follow through with the things you say?

Teachers

- How can you create a culture of high expectations in your class where every child can flourish, regardless of their background? What might this look like in terms of behaviour, routines and expectations for the standard of work that children produce? How often do you remind children about this?
- Sonia talked about the power of Quality First Teaching in improving outcomes for disadvantaged children. Have you ever accessed the EEF toolkit? If not, consider having a look at the impact summaries that synthesise the research on some significant areas of classroom practice.
- Consider your use of interventions. We know that a specific, targeted intervention can be useful when planned carefully, but do you ensure that children are not missing areas of the curriculum they are particularly enthused by? Does the person leading the intervention have the necessary subject knowledge to deliver it best?

Senior leaders

- Do you feel there is an established culture of high expectations for all children in your school? Are teachers and support staff ambitious about what disadvantaged children can achieve? If not, how can you begin to shift this culture through your CPD cycle and your systems in school?

- Considering Sonia's concept of cultural capital, how does your school enable children to share their personal 'invisible backpacks'? How do you embrace the culture and heritage of your school community?
- Is your PP grant used effectively to ensure that the CPD cycle is evidence-informed and focused on Quality First Teaching? We know that this is what makes the biggest difference to disadvantaged pupils' outcomes.

CHAPTER 8

KNOWLEDGE IS POWER

LINKED PODCAST EPISODE:
Knowledge is Power with Daisy Christodoulou and Clare Sealy

GUESTS:
Daisy Christodoulou and Clare Sealy

IN THIS CHAPTER WE EXPLORE:

- the cognitive science arguments for pupils needing knowledge stored in long-term memory;
- how knowledge enriches children's lives;
- the impact knowledge has on students' thinking skills.

ABOUT ME: DAISY CHRISTODOULOU

I am the Director of Education at No More Marking, a provider of online comparative judgement. I work closely with schools on developing new approaches to assessment. Before that, I was Head of Assessment at Ark Schools, a network of academy schools. I've taught English in two London comprehensives and have been part of government commissions on the future of teacher training and assessment.

I'm the author of *Seven Myths about Education*; *Making Good Progress?: The Future of Assessment for Learning* and *Teachers vs Tech?: The Case for an Ed Tech Revolution*.

ABOUT ME: CLARE SEALY

For the last two years I've been working as the Head of Curriculum and Standards for the states of Guernsey. Prior to that, I was the Headteacher of St Matthias Church of England Primary School in Tower Hamlets for 22 years.

During an Ofsted inspection in 2014, the lead inspector suggested that I joined Twitter. Because of that, I came into contact with a wider pool of people than would ever be possible in real life. I encountered ideas that challenged me from a range of great thinkers such as Daisy Christodoulou, Katharine Birbalsingh, David Didau and Stuart Locke. I read voraciously and a couple of years later, started writing my own blog (www.primarytimery.com). I was quite ill at the time with a lung disorder, so reading educational research and writing about it gave me something to do, since apart from going to work, I couldn't really go out. The blog took off and I was asked to speak at various conferences. Discovering a 'like mind' in primary colleague Andrew Percival (@primarypercival) was great. We went on to lead a conference about curriculum delivery for primary schools which was so successful that we ended up repeating it all over the country.

These days I am so busy with work – and so much healthier – that I don't have much time to write. But now there are a whole raft of primary colleagues writing blogs, books and making podcasts, so I feel that I have handed over the baton to a new generation, including, of course, Russell and Steve.

DAISY CHRISTODOULOU AND CLARE SEALY: THE INTERVIEW

In the summer term of 2020, we had the opportunity to engage with two of the greatest minds in education: Daisy Christodoulou and Clare Sealy. Around this time, two terrific books were released: *The researchED Guide to The Curriculum* (edited by Clare) and Daisy's book, *Teachers vs Tech?* While these books are very different, they both emphasise the value of knowledge. This interview was an opportunity to find out why Daisy and Clare are both advocates of a 'knowledge-rich' approach, and to examine the reasons why knowledge can make such a positive difference to the children in our schools.

Unfortunately, at the same time that many educators have become more vocal in their support of knowledge, this has been misinterpreted by some as a move towards a dull and lifeless school experience. As we found out when speaking to our guests, this misconception couldn't be farther from the truth. In this chapter, we will be reflecting on the key points they made about the power and beauty of knowledge, and how it is in the interest of every educator to help their students to become deeply knowledgeable.

> *Working memory is really limited, but long-term memory, by contrast, is the store of everything we have in our minds. You can't expand working memory. The only way you can cheat its limitations is to get stuff into long-term memory and use that.*

In the past few years, we have learnt a lot from cognitive science about the learning process and how memories are formed. While the debate continues as to how this knowledge should be applied to education, there are some basic principles of memory that have enormous implications for our teaching. For example, we know that our working memories are very limited and easily overloaded. We all know there is a limit to how much information any one of us can retain in working memory, and this is approximately three to five pieces of information for most people. Our long-term memory, by contrast, is a vast storehouse of memories and a very powerful lever for us to draw upon when teaching students. When we have learnt something well enough for it to become stored in long-term memory, we can solve problems with much greater ease (provided we can successfully retrieve this memory). A simple example would be how a child might use their knowledge of a particular times-table fact (stored in long-term memory) when solving a complex word problem. The fact that the child doesn't need to think very hard about the tables fact itself results in their working memory facing fewer demands, meaning they can focus on thinking about the other aspects of the problem. This suggests that it is very important for schools to make key decisions about the knowledge they want to be 'automatic' for the pupils in their care.

For some people, the focus on knowledge seems to be a waste of time. We live in a world where we can access a wealth of knowledge online, so why do children need to be knowledgeable if they can just head to their favourite search engine when they don't know something? In Daisy's book *Teachers vs Tech?*, she examines the many issues with this way of thinking. She said in the interview with us:

The mistake people make when they say 'Just Google it' is the idea that Google simply operates as an outsourced long-term memory. Actually, no: you need that long-term memory in your head; you need it because your working memory is so tiny and is really easily overwhelmed.

The idea that we can outsource our long-term memories to the internet has real implications for children's learning. What would life look like for a child who needs to refer to the internet (or any other source) constantly throughout the learning process?

Imagine reading a book where you don't know every other word. Sure, you can go look up what those words mean on Google, or in a dictionary, but how pleasant a reading experience are you going to have? How much meaning will you get from it?

In this excellent example, Daisy was highlighting how disruptive the 'Google it' mentality would be to the learners in our classrooms. As educators, we want children to be fully immersed and engaged with the book they are reading. The learning experience would be extremely unsatisfying for the young person if they needed to search for meaning outside their own minds every time they came across unfamiliar content. Far better that their long-term memory is a rich storehouse of pre-existing information, so that they are able to have a nourishing experience of reading the text.

Sometimes the perception of a 'knowledge-rich' approach is that the end-goal is getting children to simply know lots of information, and that advocates are not particularly interested in children *doing* anything with this information. In fact, the 'knowledge is power' idea is that *with* knowledge children can do the remarkable and interesting things that we want them to do (oddly often heralded as 'twenty-first century skills'). Daisy said in the podcast, 'Any kind of problem-solving you want to do relies on that body of knowledge in long-term memory', and it is pretty difficult to argue with this assertion. For example, imagine a mechanic trying to solve the problem of a faulty engine without knowing anything about cars, or imagine having to stand on a stage and deliver a speech about something you know nothing about. For too long, the idea that skills such as creativity, explaining or problem-solving are generic has led us down a real rabbit-hole. These skills are not generic and they are most certainly not twenty-first century either. Humans have been solving complex problems throughout the entirety of our evolutionary history, and we have done so consistently because of the rich body of knowledge we have acquired and passed on to future generations during this time. 'Knowledge is power' because it helps us to see and to think in ways that are truly interesting and useful.

Knowledge changes us and changes what we can see. It literally changes what we can imagine, what we are interested in, and it changes what we can think.

While the cognitive science arguments for knowledge are extremely compelling, we do a disservice to knowledge when we see it purely as a memory hack that allows us to solve interesting problems. Clearly, this is very powerful, but knowledge is much more than this; it is at the heart of what it is to be human. Clare Sealy believes passionately that knowledge itself is of great value and that it allows human beings to experience life differently. Clare has written extensively about this, and we recommend her blog 'How to speak truthfully about what it means to be human; a user's handbook', which takes this idea further. Clare made the point in the podcast that knowledge allows us to experience the true richness of life. For example, she said in the podcast: 'If you just know what trees are, that's one thing. But if you know "that's an elm, that's an oak, that's a birch . . . " instead of just seeing trees, it's changed you. You understand in a more subtle way.' We can all relate to this point when we think about a subject or topic that 'lights us up' in some way. It is in the nuances of the detail that we get excited, because knowledge is enabling us to understand that particular thing in new and illuminating ways. Being deeply knowledgeable, as opposed to knowing very little, is like the difference between seeing a pixelated image and the same image in perfect, high-definition resolution. Knowledge provides a kind of clarity, beauty and crispness to life that every student is deserving of.

That's why we need knowledge: it is the raw material of thinking.

This quotation from Clare is wonderful as it bridges the cognitive science arguments with her persuasive points about the nourishment that knowledge gives to our lives. With knowledge, we can think more deeply. Yes, that might be in order to solve problems, but it might also enable us to ponder, to imagine and to reflect. As we build a rich bank of knowledge in long-term memory, we are able to make wonderful and complex connections, referred to as 'schemas'. Daisy explained this in the podcast:

When you're building that knowledge, you are developing schemas. So you've got to stop thinking of it as isolated facts. The more you get of them, they build up these richer webs of connections and then what you're doing is making those links – those leaps across time and across subjects. That can only happen as your schema is getting richer.

Schema formation might not sound like a very romantic term for learning, but it is indeed a beautiful thing. We can often see it happening in those lightbulb moments in our classrooms when the penny drops and a child makes that mental leap between something they already know and the new content we are teaching them.

There is a healthy discussion to be had about the amount of knowledge we try to teach children versus the depth at which we want them to truly understand what we are teaching them. However, in our view, helping children to become knowledgeable individuals should be at the heart of what we do in schools. Having a rich storehouse of information in long-term memory reduces the chance of cognitive overload and gives children a greater chance of success when tackling new concepts. It also gives children the material they need to think with, enriching their experience of the world around them, and helping them to make sense of the messy and complex thing it is to be human.

RUSSELL'S REFLECTION

When it comes to the subject of knowledge, my 'road to Damascus' moment was in 2019 when I attended a conference run by Clare Sealy and Andrew Percival. Up until then, I was certainly someone who believed in generic skills and I did not value knowledge very much at all. However, during this conference I wrestled with both the cognitive science arguments and Clare's points about the beauty of knowledge, and I quickly came to realise that I had been missing something crucial about the role of schools. Indeed, another aspect that Clare and Andrew discussed was the moral argument that knowledge should be an entitlement of all children who come to school. They made the point that for many children, there wouldn't be any extra visits to libraries or museums outside school time, nor would there be a large bookcase at home for them to work through at their leisure. They made the point that every child, regardless of their background, deserves access to the same wealth of knowledge that school can provide for them. By the end of the day, I was certain that they were right about that.

I think our gut reaction to the issue of knowledge can often be informed by our own schooling experiences. I certainly received a 'generic skills' education and I think this was the cause of my initial apathy towards knowledge. I did not know very much about the world and I did not leave school with a rich storehouse of information in my long-term memory. Nevertheless, I got decent results (largely because of good coursework, I think) and went on to do well enough in life. Is the fact that I did OK with my life evidence that knowledge isn't important? Not at all. Looking back, my lack of knowledge has plagued me at various stages of my career, and in life more generally. When I went into teacher training, I remember anxiously asking on my PGCE, 'When do we learn about all the stuff we have to teach?' I was swiftly told that it was my job to brush up on subject knowledge and that they expected that we would know a lot of this content from our own schooling. This panicked me greatly and meant that I had to do extensive research during term-time to ensure that I was explaining some pretty basic stuff correctly for my pupils. How much of a better teacher might I have been if I already had rich subject-knowledge across the curriculum? How many of your weakest lessons as a teacher were because you didn't have enough clarity about the content you were teaching?

Beyond the job-related benefits of knowledge, I want to emphasise Clare's point about how knowledge enriches what you can see, think about and enjoy. Whenever I talk about knowledge, I always refer to my wife, Amy, who has a remarkable 'mind palace' of information stored in long-term memory. During our sixteen years together, I have been astonished by her knowledge of the world, how she can retain information, and her ability to make the most incredible links between subjects. She can do this because she has a rich storehouse of information in long-term memory and highly developed schemas for a whole range of topics. When it comes to knowledge acquisition, the knowledge-rich get richer and they do so more quickly than those of us who have less prior knowledge. It seems that the more you know already, the more curious it makes you, and therefore it is easier to make new connections between new and pre-existing knowledge. This is definitely the case with my wife. We can be playing Trivial Pursuit and she will be asked some obscure geography question, for example. She might not know the answer, but she will be able to make incredible mental leaps using the tiniest scrap of information and, remarkably, she will end up getting it right. Equally, Amy will often say, 'I've got no idea how I knew that' and I will sigh – enviously – wishing things could come to my mind so easily.

A while ago, with a new appreciation for knowledge, I made a conscious effort to absorb more information and to be more actively interested in remembering information. I picked a category I felt embarrassed to know very little about: flags. Yes, it's nerdy, I know. I downloaded a quizzing app and within a matter of days, I could identify dozens of new flags that had never meant anything to me before. The best bit about this wasn't simply getting a better score on the quiz, but it was realising that I could now see and understand things that meant nothing to me before. I came to develop a better understanding of which nations were predominantly Islamic because of the religious symbolism in their flags. I came to realise that certain colours were used commonly in the flags of particular continents. I became curious about other types of symbolism, such as the crane on the Ugandan flag (one of my favourite flags, by the way) which, with its raised leg, represents the forward movement of the country. I noticed things I didn't care about before, such as the day I had my attention piqued because I saw the Venezuelan flag (with its narrow arch of stars) being waved on the TV. I might not have bothered to listen before, but now I wanted to understand what was happening in that particular news article because in some small way, it meant something to me.

Knowledge changes us. It changes what we can see, what we appreciate and what we understand. We must remember that for so many children knowledge isn't going to magically find its way into their long-term memories without our help and neither will they all choose to do their own (accurate) research. It is our moral duty to give students access to a rich body of knowledge during their time with us.

STEVE'S REFLECTION

The passion from Clare and Daisy in this podcast blew me away and really got me to question some of my pre-existing ideas about teaching and learning. The fundamental crux of this episode was that deepening pupils' knowledge is a pivotal role we play as educators, and this comes hand in hand with a good understanding of working memory and long-term memory. I admit that prior to this episode this understanding was really lacking for me.

One reflection I had after the interview was that I hadn't valued knowledge enough in the past. In my case, Google had become a 'class friend'. We were fortunate to have iPads in the class and I admit it: the phrase 'If you don't know it, Google it' was something both adults and children were known to say during the school day. This episode reminded me that, as teacher, it is my role to impart the knowledge that, children need and it also caused me to question the role of technology in learning. I should say at this point that Daisy's book does not condemn technology in the classroom, but rather encourages the reader to look at how it can be used as a powerful tool for improving long-term memory, rather than out-sourcing it.

With the understanding that long-term memory is so much vaster in capacity than working memory, it became apparent that I needed to re-evaluate various aspects of my practice. It caused me to reflect on different examples about times when children in my class had struggled, purely because their long-term memories couldn't provide them with the knowledge they needed in order to tackle the tasks I was setting them.

As an experienced Upper KS2 teacher, I don't know any Year 6 teacher who wouldn't dream of every student arriving from Year 5 with a total grasp of the basics (e.g. times tables, number bonds, neat handwriting and fluent reading). However, in my experience, this isn't often the case and it is never the fault of individual teachers. Sometimes, these basics just haven't been prioritised in a systematic way so that they become secure in the long-term memories of students. These issues can then be exacerbated in Year 6, where – due to SATs pressure – we don't fully address these gaps, resulting in shallow learning in the desire to achieve good results. Hearing Clare and Daisy's discussion about knowledge was an eye-opener and made me reflect on whether my teaching, as well as the systems we had in school, were really built upon what we know about long-term memory and the value of knowledge acquisition.

Reflecting on my career, there are many examples I can think of where a lack of knowledge hindered a pupil's success. One of my Year 6 pupils had real difficulties with maths. She was able to learn the written algorithm for column addition, but her knowledge of basic addition facts was so poor that it would hinder the process dramatically. She quickly picked up the procedural steps of the algorithm, but would then invariably take 10–15 seconds to add single-digit numbers like 7 and 8, for example. This impeded her ability to solve problems, as her working memory was overloaded with focusing on the basic number facts, often causing her to lose track of where she had reached in the calculation. Unfortunately, children like this are often labelled as 'lower ability' purely because they have not memorised the facts that so much of their other learning hinges on. This podcast made me really think again about these students.

Another reflection from my time in Year 6 is about reading comprehension. The Reading SATs papers are renowned for being pretty tough, and we often get obsessed with endless comprehension tasks as a tool for addressing children's difficulties. However, after listening to Daisy speak, I became more conscious of the fact that successful comprehension was largely about knowledge, vocabulary and fluency. If these aspects of reading were seen as the highest priority from Early Years to Year 4, say, then perhaps time spent on test techniques and how to express their answers would be more useful once children were in Upper KS2. On reflection, I can think of quite a few children who I am fairly certain could not read even a hundred words a minute correctly by Year 6, and therefore this was what was holding them back from being able to comprehend the text in the SATs paper. They were sadly spending too much time thinking about the words and sounding them out, meaning that comprehension was unachievable. With greater acknowledgment of the role that long-term memory plays in reading, it made an immediate difference to my teaching and the value in creating systems that would enable children to commit these basics to long-term memory.

The concept of committing key information to long-term memory doesn't just cover the core subjects; it can be applied to everything we do in schools. I can think of times when children struggled in Geography, for example, as they were being asked to compare other areas in the world to their local area. How can children do complex tasks such as this if they don't have the prerequisite knowledge needed to do this, such as knowing about the hemispheres, different climates and key facts about where they live? Understanding the role of prior learning is fundamental to our teaching and key to pupils' schema development over time. If we do not give time for children to grasp the knowledge that they will need in future, then vital information won't even make it into long-term memory. This has huge implications for future teachers who won't be able to teach children age-appropriate material. It will be like trying to build a house upon sand.

YOUR REFLECTION

Take some time to digest what you've read during this chapter. We have provided some question prompts that you may like to consider, depending on your current role or level of experience.

Support staff

- As support staff, you play a vital role in modelling good subject knowledge for your students. Are there any areas of your current year group curriculum you need to brush up on – e.g. times tables or basic grammar terms? Your commitment to your own ongoing learning is so important for the children you support each day.
- It is very easy for teachers to forget to inform you of the upcoming learning content. Do you have a clear system in place for finding out what is about to be taught so that you are confident to deliver this alongside the teacher? If not, could you broach this with your teacher and put together a way of working that enables this to happen?
- Children will often look to you as a role model for learning behaviours. Do you think you model high levels of curiosity about new knowledge? Are there any subjects where you could do with modelling greater levels of enthusiasm or interest?

Trainee teachers

- Before going into your first ECT year, what areas of subject knowledge feel weakest for you? What work can you begin to do now so that it is not such an obstacle once you get started in your own classroom?
- During your teaching placements, how might you use the learning environment as a cue for the key knowledge children need to retain? Subject-specific terminology could be a great place to start.
- We know that children become more knowledgeable when new learning builds on prior learning. What could you do at the start of your lessons so that children always make links between old and new content?

Teachers

- Thinking about the year group you are in this year, what are the absolute essentials that children need to commit to long-term memory in order to be successful? How often will you give children time to practise these things so they become automatic? Systems are everything!
- Are you explicit enough with your students about the importance of retaining knowledge? Have you spoken to them about the dangers and limitations of relying on the internet as an information source?
- While retrieval practice hasn't been the main focus of this chapter, we know that children need lots of opportunities to revisit prior learning. How could you build in more low-stakes quizzing (and other forms of retrieval) into your daily practice?

Senior leaders

- In terms of curriculum design, to what extent do children have opportunities to revisit previously learnt knowledge over time? Is this planned out in a systematic way in every subject?
- Looking at your CPD cycle, what opportunities are there for strengthening teacher subject-knowledge in different subjects?
- What opportunities do children in your school have to share their increasing body of knowledge with others? What role could governors play in monitoring the impact of a knowledge-rich approach?

CHAPTER 9

DIFFERENTIATION

LINkED PODCAST EPISODE:
The Stuff that Matters –
Mary Myatt

GUEST:
Mary Myatt

IN THIS CHAPTER WE EXPLORE:

- the flaws associated with some forms of differentiation;
- the issues with having fixed views of pupils' ability;
- the importance of high expectations for all children;
- the vital role of scaffolding in supporting all learners to achieve.

ABOUT ME: MARY MYATT

I am an education adviser, writer and speaker. I have been working in education for nearly thirty years and originally trained as an RE teacher. I have had a number of roles in the sector, including as a local authority adviser and inspector. I love visiting schools where I get the chance to have conversations with pupils, teachers and leaders about learning, leadership and the curriculum.

I have written about leadership, school improvement and the curriculum: *High Challenge, Low Threat: How the Best Leaders Find the Balance*; *Hopeful Schools: Building Humane Communities*; *The Curriculum: Gallimaufry to Coherence*; *Back on Track: Fewer Things, Greater Depth*; *Huh: Curriculum Conversations Between Subject and Senior Leaders*. I have also established Myatt & Co, an online platform with films for teachers, including teaching assistants, and leaders, including governors.

I have been a governor in three schools and a trustee for a Multi Academy Trust. I co-founded the RE Quality Mark, am chair of the board for the Centre for Education and Youth and a member of the curriculum advisory group for Oak National Academy.

I maintain that there are no quick fixes and that great outcomes for pupils are not achieved through tick boxes.

MARY MYATT: THE INTERVIEW

What a treat it was to speak to Mary Myatt in May 2021. This interview has been one of our most popular episodes because Mary's words resonated with the lived experiences of teachers. Mary has a wonderful way of seeing through all the nonsense associated with a particular debate and gets straight to the heart of the issue. It is for this reason that we recorded an episode called 'The Stuff That Matters' which was all about getting teachers and leaders to look critically at the things we often spend so much of our time on in schools. We wanted to examine whether any of this 'stuff' needed a radical rethink, and Mary certainly had us think twice about various aspects of our work. This included things like our obsession with 'evidence', written feedback and our sector's problematic relationship with photocopying. We talked in the episode about how, as a sector, we're pretty compliant and conservative (with a small 'c'). For this reason, we generally do what is asked of us and, as a result, sometimes poor practices and lethal mutations of good ideas seep into our profession, causing damage to both teacher workload, but also outcomes for students. Mary was keen to encourage teachers and leaders to stop and ask 'why?' on a regular basis: 'Why are we doing this?' 'How will it help the young people in our care?' 'Is it sustainable?' 'Is it efficient?'

One of the most enjoyable parts of this interview was our discussion about differentiation. In this chapter, we will be reflecting on how this positive principle has morphed into some counter-productive practices in our schools. We will be considering how the good ideas behind differentiation can be delivered in such a way that means the gap in student outcomes is closed, rather than widened, over time.

> *Differentiation as an idea, in principle, is a good one, in that we make the curriculum accessible in so far as possible for every child in the classroom. What it got devolved into was 'I have got to produce different work for different groups of children'.*

When we opened up this part of the conversation, Mary was quick to acknowledge that the idea of differentiation is a positive one. Of course we want all children to access the curriculum, and we want them all to make progress, regardless of their starting points. Children have a right to have their different needs met and, as we explored in Chapter 4, it is incumbent on teachers and leaders to pre-empt and remove any potential barriers to learning. However, Mary questioned whether the way that this idea had manifested itself in our schools was actually achieving its aim. If differentiation is about helping all children to access the curriculum, then it shouldn't require teachers to set different work for different groups of children. If this is how differentiation is going to look in our schools, then it seems inevitable that we will inadvertently exacerbate the problem we are actually trying to tackle. As Mary said in the episode, 'I am busy preparing half a dozen different coloured worksheets for my class and guess what? They are going to widen gaps because I am deciding in advance what some children are capable of.' This well-meaning practice of differentiating by task is still extremely common in our schools. So what is the problem with differentiating by ability? And are these notions of ability actually reliable?

> *Why are we talking about children having low ability or teachers saying 'my lowers'? They are your children, sweetheart, they are not your lowers. All we can talk about with any confidence is prior attainment.*

At the heart of this issue is how we view the concept of ability. If we believe, as teachers and leaders, that some children are simply cleverer than other students, then this will have a huge impact on how we think about their needs and how we plan to meet them. However, if we are willing to question this notion of 'lowers', 'middles' and 'highers' and instead see ability as much more fluid and nuanced, then we will approach our planning in a very different way. Mary wasn't questioning the idea that children come to us with different levels of prior attainment. At the end of the previous year, children will have achieved different outcomes when it comes to their work and their test scores will vary greatly. However, we have a choice about the extent to which we will allow these starting points to determine the future achievement of our students.

So what do teachers mean when they talk about a child as 'low ability'? It is fairly likely that either the child has significant gaps in their learning or they just don't seem to 'get' things very quickly. In the previous chapter regarding the power of knowledge, Steve remembered a girl who had significant gaps in her addition facts, meaning she couldn't complete the written algorithm for addition very quickly. On reflection, he recognised that she wasn't incapable of doing well in maths, but she just hadn't acquired some critical knowledge that would make the whole process so much more efficient. In cases like this, it's not that the child has any kind of cognitive *inability*, but their current gaps are simply hindering what they are able to do at the moment. Worryingly, if we wrongly label children like this as 'low', then we'll end up setting them less challenging work, and the gap between them and their peers will become even greater. In the case that Steve described, this girl needed time to revisit her basic number facts, although this wouldn't be in replacement of accessing age-related material. As well as having gaps in learning, some of these so-called 'low' children may simply be individuals who think a bit differently or less quickly than their peers. This isn't necessarily a sign that they are any less capable, but they may need more processing time in order to engage fully with the material that is being presented. A simple adjustment to our practice might be giving children more thinking time when we ask a question, for example. As well as some additional thinking time, these pupils may benefit from more time to discuss the key concepts or they may need to have the information shared or explained in another way before it fully sinks in. In our race to get through the curriculum content, children like this can often be left behind or we can fall into the trap of setting them easier work for everybody's convenience.

So what is the harm in giving some children different tasks from others in lessons?

> *I find it heart-breaking that we are rationing interesting, demanding work based on what I consider to be flawed notions of ability. I don't know what a child is capable of until they are given interesting and demanding work and supported to get there.*

Mary made the case that we cannot fully know what a child is capable of until they have had the opportunity to engage with rich and challenging work. What Mary *isn't* saying is that we should give every child exactly the same work and then hope for the best that they will all perform as well as each other. She is calling on us to ensure that every pupil has the necessary support in order to access the learning material – and there are various ways we can do this. Mary's point was that it is too easy to jump to the conclusion that a child cannot do something before we have given them the opportunity to try. She believes strongly that scaffolding is the key 'differentiation' tool at every teacher's disposal. It's about pitching the work high for every child and thinking about how we support them 'up' rather than lowering our expectations. In our reflections, we will explore some different ways we can scaffold children's learning, but for Mary our most powerful classroom tool is talk.

> *Children need to be supported, I would argue, primarily through talk, in order to enter the domain with everybody else. They don't need a diminished diet.*

Mary is extremely passionate about the power of talk in supporting all children to succeed in lessons. It is something she refers to numerous times in her fantastic blog, 'Death by Differentiation', which we recommend you read. Mary was making the point that in a talk-rich classroom, the dialogue between the teacher and their pupils enables misunderstandings to be addressed there and then. Through the rich process of talking, questioning and checking for understanding, we can really support those who are struggling to succeed. It is in this dynamic, interactive environment that we are better placed to meet pupils' needs and to understand the barriers that are hindering their progress.

Once again, this is about a mentality shift on behalf of the teacher. If we enter our lessons believing (and expecting) that all children can (and will) make progress, then we are much more likely to be responsive to pupils' needs. This might be that we end up thinking more carefully about who we will target with certain questions or which students we might pop over to check on during independent practice. It might be that we choose to pair certain students together in a thoughtful way, so that someone who is more confident at explaining something is matched with someone who might benefit from their partner's explanations. When our mind-set is that all children can achieve, our teaching practices will become more precise and more intentional.

When Mary made this final point on the issue of differentiation, she referred to the fact that Ofsted's own framework talks about an ambitious curriculum for *all* children, regardless of their starting points. So while we should do nothing *for* Ofsted, it is reassuring to know that even the regulatory body for schools does not expect us to be setting different activities for different children. It is time for a big culture shift when it comes to notions of ability and effective differentiation.

RUSSELL'S REFLECTION

I cringe when I think of some of the things I did at the start of my career. In the days of 'APP grids' (Assessing Pupil Progress grids), children were set arbitrary targets based on their prior attainment. If they came to me as a '3C' I had to get them to a '3A' by the end of the year, which was expected progress. From the word go, I had a fixed idea of what children could or should achieve during their time with me. I knew intuitively that these levels could not possibly describe pupil achievement accurately and yet we were slaves to this ridiculous system. On my planning formats, I had three columns: 'HAPs', 'MAPs' and 'LAPs'. In each box, I'd identify the work that these three broad groups of children would do in my lessons. Each and every day, I quite literally planned to limit what children could achieve – and I spent hours on this nonsense.

When new assessments were introduced in 2016, there was a lot of talk about mastery. At first, many of us who were lagging behind thought mastery was the new 'higher ability' until it was broken to us that 'mastery' was, in fact, the high standard we were aiming for the vast majority of children to achieve. As a maths specialist, I tried to remain open to this idea, and it wasn't long before I really came to understand that every child had a right to reach a high standard of understanding in mathematics. Various metaphors came my way which helped me to get my head around this concept, and I'll share a couple of them now as I think they're still quite useful. One was the 'lift' analogy. Each year, your new class comes up in a lift and arrives at your year group. You then take the class on a journey through that age-appropriate curriculum and your job is to scaffold in such a way that the children stay with you on that journey. It simply isn't acceptable to let certain children 'fall out' – you have to support them to keep with you on that journey. 'Keeping them in the lift' came to mean all sorts to me and my colleagues: *explain things in smaller steps, use the right resources/representations, check for understanding and address misconceptions.* What it absolutely didn't mean was, 'give them different worksheets'. Another metaphor I heard on a maths course was a farming analogy. Someone described the idea that at the start of the year, the teacher leads their children (like sheep) into a lovely large pen. No child would be left in the previous pen, nor be allowed to head off into the next one. We'd explore that pen as a group, and of course some children would explore some corners of the field in greater depth, but we'd all get a rich experience of that pen before we headed into the next one, *together* – quite a nice analogy, I think.

So, if we are going to scaffold so that all children can access the curriculum, how might this look? Here is a list of ideas I have shared with colleagues recently. I didn't make this on my own, but drew on lots of examples I saw shared in blogs and online resources. I should particularly credit Mary Myatt for the blog we mentioned earlier, and also Ashley Booth's blog 'Dr Differentiation or: How I Learned To Stop Worrying and Love The Challenge', as each of these helped to refine my thinking.

1. **Break the lesson into small chunks**

   Break a lesson into a series of 'mini-lessons' that gradually moves students towards deeper understanding. For example, a challenging maths problem might be broken up into several parts that are taught successively. Between each mini-lesson, the teacher checks to see if students have understood the key concepts and gives them time to practise before moving on to the next step.

2. **Modelling (including live modelling)**

   Children are given a model example of a task they will be asked to complete. The teacher describes the exemplar's features and why it is of a high standard. Similarly, a teacher may also live model the process – for example, a piece of writing – so that the children can see how each step is done before they are asked to do it themselves.

3. **Pre-teaching**

Children are given a mini-input/lesson before the main lesson. The teacher/TA reviews the vocabulary or concepts the children might struggle with to increase the likelihood of them accessing the future lesson successfully.

4. **Step-by-step instructions/guides (e.g. structure strips)**

The teacher gives clear directions that the children need to follow. A handout may show these steps as a visual reminder to relieve cognitive load.

5. **Explicitly link to prior learning**

The teacher explicitly describes how the new lesson builds on the knowledge and skills that students were taught in a previous lesson. By doing this, the teacher supports effective schema development.

6. **Valuing talk**

Quality talk can scaffold the learning by helping children to generate ideas and clarify their thinking. When accompanied by helpful notes/images, the essence of the discussion can be captured and displayed as a reminder for the children when completing their work.

7. **Check for understanding**

Anticipate key points in the lesson when children may begin to struggle and build in opportunities to reclarify the task and/or share good examples in the class that others can learn from.

8. **Use of additional visuals/concrete apparatus**

A carefully selected graphic or image can support children to connect ideas. If some children struggle with 'holding' information in their short-term memory, meaningful visuals can help act as cues when they are completing their work.

This isn't an exhaustive list of scaffolding techniques, but I think it's a good start. Remember that a good scaffold can be slowly removed over time as children gain confidence.

My final point on this matter is that if you choose to ban the terms 'lower' or 'higher' ability, don't replace them with other euphemisms. When I first spoke about maths mastery to some colleagues, I remember acknowledging that some children spotted patterns more quickly, and I mentioned that I'd heard these children referred to as 'rapid graspers' in some training I'd attended. Before I knew it, I discovered that the term 'non-rapid graspers' had made its way into my school! If we find ourselves using new labels to mean 'low ability', then I suggest that we've perhaps somewhat missed the point.

STEVE'S REFLECTION

First, what a pleasure it was to chat with such a wonderful guest about the stuff that truly matters. Differentiation is a thought-provoking topic and my understanding of it has evolved greatly as I have become more aware of what it really is. The issue of differentiating via 'multiple-coloured worksheets' for your 'top, middle and lowers' really brought home the damage some forms of differentiation can do, inadvertently putting a ceiling on what children can achieve.

When I completed my PGCE, I had an awareness of what differentiation meant in the primary context, and it quickly became apparent how I was expected to apply this in my teaching. You would start the academic year with a class list (and their prior attainment grades) and you would group the children accordingly. If you were lucky, it would balance out to be fairly equal-sized groups of children – enough children to seat on each table of four to six pupils preferably. This arrangement would lead to having a group of hard-working 'higher children' (you know, the ones who would shout out the answers to every question, but would always be dependable in an observation to give the right answer). Then you would have the silent majority of 'middlies' (maybe two or three groups of them) who would crack on with the work, but who would always be out of reach of the 'highers'. And then, finally, you'd have a group of around six children who would sit on one table (usually at the front) and these would be your 'lowers'. These children would need a different worksheet as they wouldn't be able to grasp the teaching input properly and would need further support to complete their work. If you were lucky, you may even have the children sitting at the same tables for both English and maths. Looking back, how wrong was this model of differentiation? I am really grateful that my first class actually made pretty good progress, despite the way I structured my lessons back then. I even had the groups scribbled up on large posters so they all knew where they were, and every term children knew that they might be lucky enough to move up (or sadly, sometimes down) a group. What on earth was I doing? I suspect I am not alone in having taught this way during one stage of my career, and I would guess that this may still be common practice in many classes today.

The conversation with Mary was enlightening and provided clarity about what differentiation is. Sadly, what I described as my practice was a classic lethal mutation of a good idea. In my desire to support each learner, I was in fact simply rationing challenging work for the children. I hoped the 'highs' would just get the tough stuff, the 'middle ability' would do well enough (perhaps they'd sometimes extend themselves to the work the 'highers' began with) and then my Teaching Assistant would work with the 'lower ability children' to support them to, well, survive mainly. This short-sighted and damaging set-up simply gave most children a diminished diet of work and I am so glad it isn't reflective of how I now work, both as a teacher and school leader.

As Mary said in the podcast, many children who are low prior attainers are also on the pupil premium list. It can't possibly be that their innate ability is determined by their post-code, but it is most certainly the case that we can exacerbate this problem by keeping children locked within the 'attainment groups' they come to us in. To avoid this trap, we have to give all children exposure to the same curriculum content. This doesn't mean taking certain children outside the classroom to constantly work in small groups, but instead it is about removing the barriers that are hindering them from accessing the rich and challenging work. Russell spoke about some different forms of scaffolding we can use in class and by having a mastery approach to our lesson design, we enable all children to 'stay in the lift'.

Yes, some children will work a bit faster and perhaps go a bit deeper with their understanding. But we have to believe that all children can access their age-related curriculum content with the right support.

While prior attainment groups are useful to know about, we have to remember that they aren't indicative of children's performance in all areas or even within a specific subject. Just because a pupil didn't achieve very well on an end-of-year maths assessment that doesn't mean they are weak in all areas of mathematics, nor does it mean that this individual will be a weak reader, scientist, geographer or sportsperson, so labelling any child as 'lower' is wholly unhelpful. I loved it when Mary said: 'They are your children, sweetheart, not your lowers'. This is it! Children are so much more than the grades or scores they come to us with; they are wonderful little people with so much potential. We need to shift the language we use about children and talk more positively about the potential of every individual. Conversations between staff about pupils occur on a daily basis. I would hope that more teachers will become brave in challenging limiting descriptions of what pupils can do when they hear colleagues talking a pupil down. In the same way that we wouldn't see it as acceptable to talk about colleagues as 'stronger' or 'weaker' teachers, we should not speak in this way about our students.

I can safely say that Mary's thoughts on differentiation really made me reflect on how I can provide the very best educational diet for the children in my care. Not only will I not be wasting time in future creating different worksheets for different groups of children, I will also be in the Business Manager's good books for not spending such a fortune on unnecessary photocopying!

YOUR REFLECTION

Take some time to digest what you've read during this chapter. We have provided some question prompts that you may like to consider, depending on your current role or level of experience.

Support staff

- When working with a group of children, remember you are there to scaffold their success, rather than operating as an overly 'helpful hand'. How can you use questioning and modelling to support these children, rather than allowing them to simply lean on you for answers?
- Do you find you are often sitting with the same children? Could you have a conversation with the class teacher about varying which children you support in order to avoid 'learnt helplessness' kicking in?
- The language you and the class teacher use about children can inadvertently reinforce ideas about fixed ability. Do you ever use terms such as 'the lowers'? How could this change so that we don't fall into the trap of negative labelling?

Trainee teachers

- On placements, look at how the existing class teacher chooses to group their children. Is it always by a fixed notion of ability or is it more fluid? What seems to work best for the children (rather than what is most convenient for the adults)?
- When in schools, talk to other professionals about the children you are working with. What tips can you pick up about how to help children who you are finding it tricky to scaffold for? There will be a wealth of knowledge you can draw upon from experienced teachers and support staff.
- When you are making and preparing resources, how can you ensure that tasks are rich, meaning that they give *all* children the chance to think deeply and meaningfully about the content you are teaching?

Teachers

- When you inherit a new class, you will inevitably receive historical data for your pupils. How can you ensure that you have an ambitious view of the progress every child can make with you, regardless of their starting points? It's important that this prior attainment doesn't limit your view of their future achievement.
- In this chapter, we recognised that 'ability' is a nuanced issue and all children have strengths in different areas. To what extent do you seek out and celebrate these different strengths in your classroom?
- How could the mastery practices you use in maths lessons be extended to your lessons in the wider curriculum – e.g. are tasks 'low threshold, high ceiling' in nature? Are children given scaffolds to support their success or are they limited by unchallenging and closed tasks?

Senior leaders

- Have you done any whole-staff training about your vision for differentiation at your school? Within this, you will need to look at the language that staff use about children and why scaffolding enables all children to be stretched and challenged appropriately. Remember those great blogs from Mary Myatt and Ashley Booth.
- It is likely, even with training from you, that some staff may have a fixed view about the benefits of traditional differentiation. How might you challenge this in such a way that colleagues are willing to make changes to their practice? Can you point them to good examples of scaffolding working successfully within the school?
- When you observe teaching in school, do you see that teachers have high expectations for what every child in their class can achieve? Is this reflected in their questions, their resources and their use of additional adult support? If it isn't, what can be done to shift this culture?

CHAPTER 10

BEING EVIDENCE-INFORMED

LINKED PODCAST EPISODE:
The Evidence-informed Teacher
with Kathryn Morgan

GUESTS:
Kathryn Morgan

IN THIS CHAPTER WE EXPLORE:

- why being evidence-informed is critical for every teacher;
- how we can access evidence and curate our own CPD libraries;
- the importance of understanding your own context;
- keeping a critical lens and being wary of lethal mutations.

ABOUT ME: KATHRYN MORGAN

After university, I completed my PGCE in Primary Education at the University of Birmingham and started my NQT year serving a disadvantaged community in north Solihull. The school had been in difficulty for much time and ended up in special measures in my first year of teaching. While this made my induction into teaching even harder, it also helped me to see just how integral ongoing, quality professional development was for teachers' practice and students' learning.

From there, I went on to be a middle leader in a successful junior school and was fortunate to work in a high-performing environment that really valued teacher and leadership development. Although it too served a disadvantaged community, it was one of the top performing schools in the borough. I then went on to serve as a middle leader in a large, four-form entry Birmingham primary school before moving back to north Solihull as an Assistant Head in the first instance, and then as a Deputy Head for Teaching and Learning, and Professional Development. Once again, I found myself serving a disadvantaged community and a school in need of significant improvement. We heavily invested in CPD and ensured that high-quality professional development was at the heart of our school improvement plans.

After Solihull, I went on to be Director of Professional Learning at a small Multi-Academy Trust serving some of Birmingham's most deprived communities and then on to be Associate Dean in Learning Design at Ambition Institute. Following this, I worked for the Teacher Development Trust, the national charity for teacher and leader CPD, before recently starting a new role as Capacity Improvement Advisor at The Teaching School Hub Council. I am also studying for a Master's in Educational Leadership.

KATHRYN MORGAN: THE INTERVIEW

After two years of podcasting, we became significantly more interested in the subject of evidence-informed practice. We had spoken to many brilliant leaders and educational authors who had referred to the importance of evidence within their work in schools. Through our Facebook group and Twitter account, we had noticed that many more teachers seemed to have become interested in evidence-informed practice, and yet we were aware that this was probably largely dependent on their specific school contexts and cultures. It is our view that *all* teachers have the right (and duty) to become evidence-informed practition-ers, and while school leaders have a huge part to play in this, we want this chapter to highlight the fact that *any* teacher can take some ownership of their professional develop-ment and learning.

In the winter of 2020, we spoke to the wonderfully insightful Kathryn Morgan, whose career has been guided and inspired by educational research and the evidence about the best bets regarding effective classroom practice. This episode aimed to unpick why it was important to become an evidence-informed teacher and how those who are interested could learn more if they wanted to. Kathryn gave so much sound advice on this topic, and if you happen to be a school leader, we strongly recommend you listen to the full episode if you are interested in how you might implement an evidence-informed culture in your school.

> *We tend to develop teaching pedagogy and practice based on our own learning experiences . . . We can quickly pick up habits that are not grounded in evidence and can actually be detrimental to student learning.*

Without evidence, how do teachers make decisions about what they do each and every day in the classroom? As Kathryn said in the podcast, your approaches are likely to be largely informed by what kind of schooling experiences you have had throughout your life. Other influences might include what you have observed other teachers doing, what schools you have taught in, and simply what you *like* doing the most. These influences may seem harm-less enough, but what if you have picked up some habits that are not only ineffective, but actually detrimental to pupils' learning? Imagine if there was even one small aspect of your practice that you do *every single day* that holds children back, and yet you are completely unaware of it being an issue. Being evidence-informed isn't about being the 'perfect' teacher (thankfully, they don't exist), but it is about being highly reflective and willing to learn about the strategies and approaches that are most likely to benefit the students in your care. These approaches are often referred to as 'best bets' – a helpful phrase to use when discussing evidence-informed strategies.

> *We have hugely limited resources, both in terms of time and money, and we just can't afford to waste valuable learning time on pedagogy and practice that is not evidence-informed.*

So why should teachers bother to become more evidence-informed? Aren't we busy enough already? Don't we know enough about what works from our own experiences in the class-room? In the podcast, Kathryn was clear that while experience is important, without evidence, *every* teacher is prone to implementing strategies that are ineffectual. When we were discussing this, she said: 'We would be really hard-pushed to find any teacher in our sector who hasn't done crazy things, but with the very best of intentions.' We shall reflect on our own examples of this later, but the point here is that time is precious in education and we can't afford to ignore the evidence about what is or isn't likely to work – our students deserve better. A huge body of educational research, carried out over many years and in a wide range of contexts, is available. Thanks to organisations such as the Education Endowment Foundation (EEF), the busy teacher can access this information in a way that has been synthesised and summarised for our convenience. So while some teachers may choose to go further and read the original research in its 'purest' form, there are people who have done a lot of the leg-work for us already. Over time, we can build up our individual understanding of authors and organisations who we particularly trust when it comes to communicating the findings of educational research.

In the podcast, Kathryn mentioned one of the authors who has challenged some long-lasting educational myths. She talked about Daisy Christodoulou, whose brilliant book *Seven Myths About Education* critiqued a lot of educational orthodoxy. Drawing upon her own reading and learning, Daisy's book challenges ideas (many we were taught, such as 'teacher-led instruction is passive') with reference to the principles of modern cognitive science. By engaging with texts such as this, teachers can develop a more critical lens and challenge ideas that are unlikely to improve outcomes for their students.

Before moving on, we want to be clear that teachers do not have to blindly accept the work of educational writers, podcasters or bloggers. However, by engaging critically with respected thinkers like Daisy (who have engaged heavily with educational research), we can begin to improve our own knowledge of the evidence that is available to us.

> *We need to make sure that we are making more evidence-informed choices, but then also making those choices through the lens of our own context and culture . . . it is a blending of the two.*

A great point that Kathryn was keen to emphasise was that we have to combine our knowledge of the evidence with our valuable knowledge of our specific contexts. We can't replicate research exactly, because every classroom, school and community is unique. What this means is that teachers have to engage with evidence, but also to have a degree of flexibility as to what it will look like in their classrooms. For example, a teacher might read a book about the power of retrieval practice (which has a strong grounding in evidence) and decide to try out some strategies in their classroom. They might discover that some of the strategies seem to work well and some perhaps not so much. This could be for a whole host of reasons, including how well the strategies are implemented, the age of the children or what other experiences the children have had of retrieval practice in the past. This is why we need to see the idea of 'evidence-informed' as a continual journey of reflection, rather than a destination. You'll never wake up one day and realise you've 'nailed it', but you can commit to a career of learning and a willingness to adapt your practice based on your students' needs.

> *Start to curate your own library that you can dip in and out of . . . if you can build up your own library – irrespective of what your school culture is like – then I think that is only going to be positive.*

Some teachers may be very fortunate and find themselves working in schools where evidence is spoken about regularly, and where leaders filter useful blogs, videos, podcasts and books their way. However, this is unlikely to be the case for all teachers and Kathryn was keen to emphasise that becoming evidence-informed can be very much teacher-led and empowering for the practitioner. By engaging with websites such as Twitter, teachers can build their own networks which allow them to discover new ways to engage with the evidence that is out there. Clearly, this requires a very critical eye, but over time teachers can curate their own collection of 'go-to' people in education who they trust and respect. This is definitely the case for us. As we have become more experienced in engaging with Twitter, we have learnt to recognise when we spot a teacher, leader or author whose thinking is grounded in evidence. If you look through our history of podcast guests, you will notice that most of these people have written blogs, books or have been interviewed by others beforehand. This has enabled us to do our own form of 'quality assurance' before inviting them on to the podcast. It is also about recognising that different educators have different specialisms. For example, we will always go to someone like John Walker (Director of Sounds-Write) if we want guidance about phonics, because we have huge admiration for the knowledge he has accumulated through many years of working in that specific field. Equally, we have dozens of 'go-to' people for just about every other education category you can think of, whether that be Early Years, leadership or the curriculum, for example.

In Kathryn's case, one thing she has done is to develop her own simple Excel spreadsheet with tabs for the different themes she is interested in. When she has listened to or read something of interest, she adds it in and saves the file. Over time, she has curated her own personal bank of links to which she can return whenever she wants to or needs to. What a great idea and something *anyone* can do, regardless of their role or experience level.

> *Lethal mutations are where we take a piece of research and do a very surface level reading, think we understand, and apply it in our own setting, but without fidelity. We don't stay true to the active ingredients that made that research powerful in the first place.*

The final point we wanted to reflect on was this idea of 'lethal mutations', something Dylan Wiliam and many others have referred to. It is worth teachers being aware of this potential problem when they begin to engage more broadly with the work of educational writers and thinkers. As Kathryn explained so eloquently, this issue is about adopting a (good) idea in a very surface-level way and then implementing it without fidelity – that is, the teacher hasn't developed a thorough enough understanding of the strategy and its evidence-base, so it morphs into something different from what it was intended to be. Unsurprisingly, the results of the strategy are likely to be unfruitful, and this can be a huge cause of frustration for both teachers and leaders who thought they were engaging positively with the evidence.

We really like the term 'active ingredients', which are in essence the key components that make the strategy more likely to work. This is often the bit we can overlook in our haste to try out new things, yet without these ingredients we are likely to waste a lot of time and energy. If we return again to the idea of retrieval practice, for example, it is an area where there are dozens of strategies you could try, but very few of these are likely to be effective if the teacher hasn't grasped why retrieval practice is so important and what its important features are. If you were keen to try out retrieval practice in your classroom, you would need to have a strong sense of the principles that will make it effective. For example, are all children involved in the process? If you weren't able to understand the importance of this particular principle, then you may slip into implementing it in a way that encourages only *some* of your students to think. This is likely to be demoralising for you, ineffective for some of the students, and you may end up abandoning a good idea prematurely.

Becoming an evidence-informed educator is about a life-long commitment to learning. It's not about devaluing your lived experiences or professional judgement, but it's about recognising that you do one of the most sophisticated and difficult jobs imaginable. In our view, given the complexity of the task in hand, we'd be absolutely mad not to engage with the wealth of evidence that is available to our profession.

RUSSELL'S REFLECTION

We talked in Chapter 8 about the power of knowledge, and this couldn't be truer when it comes to becoming an evidence-informed teacher. As teachers and school leaders, we can only make decisions based on what we already know, and we're really limiting our impact if we don't engage with the evidence that is available to us. I agreed with Kathryn when she said that we simply don't have the time to waste on ineffective practices. I want to know that my school is focusing its energies on the strategies that are most likely to support our students to succeed. Coming back to the point made in the chapter about disadvantaged students: it really is these children who get the toughest deal when we refuse to acknowledge the evidence that is available about effective teaching.

One of the greatest benefits of becoming more evidence-informed is being liberated from the 'magpie effect' that I used to be prone to – that is, being drawn towards something because it's 'shiny'. This happened frequently throughout the first eight years of my career. For example, I remember being very drawn to fancy resources that had a novelty factor to them, but often these would take hours to prepare, only to be used once or twice in the classroom. I simply hadn't realised that my time would have been so much better spent on something like improving my subject knowledge or planning my questions carefully. As a leader, I have been guilty of the magpie effect too, running staff meetings about how teachers could use a particular piece of technology for assessment, for example. Looking back, it's not that the idea was particularly awful, but I would have been so much better spending this time supporting colleagues to hone their questioning skills, something that would have a high impact and that they were much more likely to use on a daily basis. Becoming more evidence-informed has made me become much more selective and careful about what I bring into my school, and I think that is a very healthy thing.

The critical lens that being evidence-informed gives you is also extremely empowering. It means that when a strategy comes your way you can stop and consider whether it fits with what you know about effective practice. I have spoken to various teachers who have used evidence-informed blogs or books to discuss issues with their senior leadership teams, for example. I learnt of a teacher who was demoralised by their school's archaic marking policy in which, basically, they were expected to write extensive amounts in children's books. The outdated policy was based on a misunderstanding about effective feedback, so the teacher chose to do some reading about this issue. They came across the brilliant blog 'No Written Marking. Job Done' by Deputy Headteacher Andrew Percival, which considers this issue in a critical and objective way. In the blog, Andrew reflects on the research and evaluates some of the work from the respected educational thinkers that prompted him to rewrite his policy. He then talks through his school's revised approach to marking and feedback in a way that is really easy to understand. With this brilliant blog to hand, the teacher was able to take this to their leadership team and propose a potential alternative. They were then given licence to trial a new approach in their classroom – what a great result for the staff and children.

One of the greatest barriers to becoming a more evidence-informed teacher is time. From a leadership perspective, this really chimed for me during the first national lockdown. Unlike later lockdowns when remote learning absorbed every minute of the day, the first lockdown seemed to slow time down a little and many teachers had a tiny bit more headspace than they had before March 2020. What I noticed during this time was that many people, including my own colleagues, became really keen to do more professional learning – they read more blogs, did more online courses and listened to more podcasts. I remember how the listening figures for our podcast seemed to boom during that time and it was then that I realised just how much teachers and leaders want to keep learning. However, in the normal 'madness' of everyday school life, many teachers simply can't find the headspace to engage with educational research or evidence-informed literature. Realising this issue in my own setting, we became determined to build in more time within our CPD cycle for teachers to engage with some educational books. Twice a half term, we have staff meetings based on a particular educational text (such as *Teaching WalkThrus* by Tom Sherrington and Oliver Caviglioli). By carving out this precious time, teachers are able to slow down, to read and to discuss their practice. We often complement these sessions with other great blogs that support the theme being discussed. I appreciate this is frustrating for teachers who aren't given this time. What I would say to you is to find a small way to make it work for you and your circumstances. I know many teachers who just listen to the odd podcast – perhaps on a drive to work or during a run once a week. I know others who pop onto Twitter occasionally and read the odd blog. It might not seem like much, but I have found that this interest often snowballs and ends up highlighting other great blogs and podcasts that teachers choose to tuck into at a later date.

STEVE'S REFLECTION

I don't know about you, but 'evidence-informed practice' wasn't something I'd got to grips with until recently, and I really wish I had sooner. Over ten years ago, I remember attending regular NQT district meetings and being fortunate to go on some very 'jazzy' courses. I remember in particular being told about different 'learning styles' and how I could shoehorn in various bits of technology so everyone could access my teaching. There was very little back then about blogs, podcasts and online CPD, and vlogs were unheard of. Times have changed, however, and I consider us to be extremely fortunate with what is now available to support us in our jobs. However, this comes with a significant health warning: not everything out there is tailored for your setting or rooted in evidence, so while there is so much good to support us, we must keep that critical lens on at all times.

In our chat with Kathryn, it was warming to hear that teachers have to be able to make mistakes on the path to becoming more evidence-informed. Heck, when I reflect on my teaching career I can think of numerous times where I tried something I had read about and it didn't quite seem to work as I had hoped. My main issue was sometimes taking an idea but implementing it very superficially – basically just scratching the surface. For example, I remember reading so much about the importance of developing a 'growth mindset' culture, and I jumped straight onto that particular bandwagon. I bought posters galore with inspirational phrases, we developed a huge 3D display on growth mindset, and it became a key theme for our assemblies, backed up with superficial YouTube videos and songs. But this was not enough for it to have a significant impact. Sure, talking about growth mindset helped our children to become more positive about their learning, but did we go deep enough into Carol Dweck's original thinking and critically evaluate how it could or should look in our school? Looking back, the idea required more research from leaders and better CPD for staff. We needed to be clear on its purpose and to communicate this better with all stakeholders so that the children and families also understood its intended purpose.

This leads me to the concept of 'fads'. I think we have all been there: we attend a course and marvel over something that is new, shiny and seems to be a silver bullet. I have walked away from courses thinking that I couldn't wait to get a 'new idea' implemented, and yet often nothing really materialises. Perhaps the idea is too expensive, it needs too many people involved, or it's simply not right. On the flip-side, many of you will have witnessed a new, rushed initiative brought in by leaders with the best of intentions. Unfortunately, without enough thought, these can often become new 'tick-box' exercises that are not evidence-informed in the slightest. This is why I feel Kathryn was spot-on when she discussed developing a critical eye, and the benefits of building your own CPD library that you can dip in and out of. With so much at our fingertips, there are many ways to become more evidence-informed. This might be via podcasts (our one in particular, of course!), blogs, vlogs and websites such as the EEF Toolkit, which synthesises a lot of the research in a way that is easy for the busy teacher to access and engage with. I have had the privilege of working with teachers who have curated their own CPD libraries, and it is incredibly empowering for them. When numerous teachers in a school begin to engage with evidence, it creates a culture where you can all learn more collaboratively, too.

I remember beginning my teaching career with 'all-singing, all-dancing' lessons, spending hundreds of pounds on jazzy resources and having highly stimulating classrooms. I think my partner came in once and said, 'Wow, it looks like someone has vomited resources over your walls'. I thought that the more I did, the better it was for the children, and I had read somewhere about children needing to see key vocabulary everywhere for it to sink in. The reality was that I was putting far too much up, and it was more like gaudy wallpaper rather than a learning aid. In terms of my teaching, I was also encouraged to do no more than 20 per cent of the talk in any lessons, which I now know is not supported at all by the evidence. Many years into my career, I had the pleasure of teaching a class with high levels of SEND who had many behaviour challenges too. Being a little more evidence-informed by this stage, I knew both the value of considering the specific context of my class, as well as recognising the benefits of more direct instruction as a teaching approach. With this particular class, they needed a really *unstimulating* environment, free from distractions. In this kind of classroom they could focus better, whereas other classes I had taught in the past could cope with a little more stuff on the walls. These children also really benefited from lots of direct instruction and way more modelling from me than I had ever done with classes before. So what I am saying is that considering those 'best bets' about what the evidence says is most likely to work in the classroom, but then adapt these ideas based on your specific context. As teachers, we have to be willing to constantly tweak what we do to meet the needs of the children in front of us.

In summary, be critical of things you see online, look into ideas further and consider curating your own CPD library. Remember that it is impossible to exactly replicate the research in your own class, because you can never re-create the exact conditions under which the original research was conducted. However, engage with the evidence and take a nuanced approach, considering your own set of complex circumstances. Every step you take towards being a more evidence-informed teacher has the potential to improve the outcomes for the students in your care.

YOUR REFLECTION

Take some time to digest what you've read during this chapter. We have provided some question prompts that you may like to consider, depending on your current role or level of experience.

Support staff

- Is there a particular teacher or leader in your school who might be able to signpost you to CPD materials to read or watch? This can be a good starting point for becoming more evidence-informed.
- Have you considered starting your own Twitter account in order to engage with other educational thinkers? You may find that by reaching out in this way you can begin to curate your own CPD.
- If you go to the EEF website, you can search for 'Making Best Use of Teaching Assistants', which discusses the evidence about how support staff can best be used within schools. How might this support the valuable work you do in schools each day?

Trainee teachers

- Are you aware of where support can be provided online in terms of being more evidence-informed? Remember to keep a critical lens – not every piece of advice will be robust. However, over time you will develop more confidence in who you can go to for different areas of specialism. Twitter is great for this.
- Consider the points made about 'fads' in this chapter. Have you noticed yourself or others being drawn into approaches that are not based on evidence? Can you think of a resource or approach that was based on its 'fun' appeal, rather than the impact it would have on learning?
- When visiting prospective schools, why not ask about the evidence-informed culture? Do leaders encourage their staff to become more evidence-informed? If so, how do they facilitate this?

Teachers

- When you engage with evidence, remember the importance of those 'active ingredients'. Do you always make sure you understand the 'why' behind the strategy? What principles need to be in place for the technique/strategy to work?
- Remember to combine evidence with your knowledge of your own context. When trying out a new approach, do you always give yourself time to tweak and refine a technique before giving up or trying something different? It's all about engaging with the evidence but adapting it to work within your context.
- When you discover a new educational book, blog or podcast, do you think to share this with colleagues? Sometimes this is just as powerful for developing an evidence-informed culture as when leaders introduce materials to staff.

Senior leaders

- What time is carved out for both teachers and support staff to talk about evidence-informed approaches? If this time is not provided, then staff are unlikely to have the headspace to think about evidence-informed practice.
- Is there a place in the school building where teachers can access and share evidence-informed approaches – e.g. a CPD library or display in the staffroom? These strategies can be part of a wider culture shift to becoming more evidence-informed.
- What time do you give yourself to engage with the evidence about education? You need to model a culture where your decision-making is based on robust evidence, rather than on your own personal preferences.

CHAPTER 11

IN SUMMARY

We want to thank every podcast guest we have had on since 2018 for enabling us to become better teachers, better leaders and, importantly, better people. Speaking to every one of you has enriched our lives, meaning that the podcast has never felt like a chore, but always such a treat. Picking ten episodes to focus on for this book was an almost impossible task, and we are hopeful that in future we may be able to write about many more of the wonderful people we have talked to since the podcast was first launched.

In picking ten themes for our book, we knew that we wouldn't be able to say *everything* there is to say about each theme, and nor have we attempted to. For each topic that we chose to write about, there exists a whole number of inspiring books you may now want to go on and read. What we aimed to do in this book was to capture how each of these inspiring guests led us into a deeper place of understanding and how their insights helped us to refine what we were doing in our own schools. We really hope that our personal learning has in some way benefited you, too, and in some way uplifted or inspired you. Perhaps some of the chapters have triggered a particular interest in you or made you want to learn more. If not, at least you've got yourself a very nice-looking coaster or an effective fly-swatter at least.

Throughout the writing process, we have often talked about how overwhelming and terrifying it has all been. While we are very proud of our podcast, we're conscious that we're just two Deputy Heads doing our best to support our colleagues, students and school communities. We're not prominent researchers or renowned educational writers, but we have really tried to write this book from an honest and personal space, and we hope that has shone through for you while reading. We're grateful to SAGE Publishing and to Amy Thornton for seeing the potential in our ideas.

We want to acknowledge every person who has taken a punt on us, who has supported the podcast and who chose to buy this book. You are part of the most incredible profession in the world, and what you do for young people each and every day is quite astonishing. Due to you today, a child may well have:

- smiled;
- laughed;
- become wiser;
- developed more empathy;
- understood a concept;
- felt loved;
- felt supported;
- felt special;
- grown in self-belief;
- been able to express their feelings for the very first time.

The list could go on. Thank you for being everyday heroes.

Finally, we would like to thank a few other people for their support.

FROM RUSSELL

- A huge thank you to my wife, Amy, and our daughters Imelda and Juno. Many weekends and holidays have been part-absorbed by this book and I am so grateful for your patience during this past year. I love you all so much.
- Thank you to my amazing family based in Essex. I wouldn't have had this opportunity if it wasn't for the consistent love and support you have given me throughout my life.
- I'm so grateful to my colleagues at Willowbrook who always seem to back me, even when I'm doubting myself. I have an incredible Senior Leadership team who have been nothing but supportive, and a team of teachers and TAs I could only have dreamed of working with.
- I want to extend a special thank you to Liz and Stu, who we featured in the book. You have helped me to recognise my potential and to understand how my mind works. This has been life-affirming and truly transformative.
- Oh, and I'd better thank Steve, I suppose – a close and trusted friend. You mean the world to me and I'm so glad we've done this together. It's amazing to write a book, but it's even cooler to share the journey with such an awesome dude. Cheers, buddy.

FROM STEVE

- Without question, my first thank you has to be to my partner, Laura, who actually enabled me to write this book (and record many podcasts). Without her continued support and confidence (and looking after Everly while I snuck off for writing time), I would never have been able to give the necessary time and passion this deserves. Thanks also to Amy and Rhys who have to hear me bang on about our podcast and trying to convince them to listen – although they never will!
- Thanks to my mum and dad who are my idols. Their work ethic, positivity and support has inspired me to be the best I can be and to try new things, like creating our Facebook group and starting a podcast. My mum was the person who got me into teaching, so thank you for that, and my dad didn't moan as much as I thought he might have when I left life as a lawyer!
- Thanks also to the fantastic colleagues I have worked with over the last ten years. I have learnt so much from you all and I am grateful to you for allowing me to talk about the podcast at school. I appreciate you all joining the Facebook group and for putting up with me talking about podcast guests and new ideas all the time. Thanks to the SLT for never outwardly 'poo-pooing' my enthusiasm or heckling me in staff meetings!
- Lastly, thanks Russell. I haven't put you last because you put me last (promise), but because I literally could not have done any of this without you. The podcast may be our joint venture, but it is also your baby and you work so hard to make it the joy it is. Thanks, pal. We may be on opposite sides of the country, but you would never know. At least Laura doesn't think so, as my phone is always pinging from our conversations! Top work, my friend. I would never want to do it with anyone else. Smashed it!

INDEX